The Oryx Multicultural Folktale Series

A Knock at the Door

by
George Shannon

Illustrated by
Joanne Caroselli

ORYX PRESS
1992

The rare Arabian Oryx is believed to have inspired the myth of the unicorn. This desert antelope became virtually extinct in the early 1960s. At that time several groups of international conservationists arranged to have 9 animals sent to the Phoenix Zoo to be the nucleus of a captive breeding herd. Today the Oryx population is nearly 800, and over 400 have been returned to reserves in the Middle East.

Copyright © 1992 by The Oryx Press
4041 North Central at Indian School Road
Phoenix, Arizona 85012-3397

Published simultaneously in Canada

∞ The paper used in this publication meets the minimum requirements of American National Standard for Information Science—Permanence of Paper for Printed Library Materials, ANSI Z39.48, 1984.

A list of copyright statements for contributed material appears on page ix and x.

Library of Congress Cataloging-in-Publication Data
A Knock at the door / [compiled] by George Shannon.
    p. cm. — (The Oryx multicultural folktale series)
  Includes bibliographical references and index.
  Summary: A collection of thirty-five versions, representing countries and cultures from around the world, of the traditional tale in which a dangerous character knocks at the door and tries to trick the children inside into letting him in. Includes information about the tales, related activities, and resources.
  ISBN 0-89774-733-X (alk. paper)
  1. Fairy tales. [1. Fairy tales. 2. Folklore.] I Shannon, George.   II. Series.
PZ8.K75   1992
[398.21]—dc20
                                                        92-1714
                                                          CIP
                                                          AC

Stories are an actual participation in the art of living. Listening to a story, learning it, and telling it to other people are all part of one experience—the experience of personal involvement in existence.

John Mbiti
Akamba Stories

To
Shirley T. Lastwin

Contents

Preface

"The more things change," so the adage goes, "the more they stay the same." It is especially true with folktales and the truths they share. For example, here in the Midwest, flyers prepared by one religious sect warning against another have recently begun appearing on local bulletin boards. They alert the unsuspecting about proselytizers who knock at their door. They may *seem* like you, state the flyers, but they are not and only want to upset your home and harm your children. They *appear* to be good, but they are actually evil. In a lighter vein, one of the most popular running skits on the original *Saturday Night Live* television program was the "land shark" who knocked on doors in hopes of dinner. People always asked who he was before opening the door, but it never helped. The shark would soften his voice, pretending to be someone warm and friendly like the candy-gram delivery boy. Convinced of their safety the people would open the door only to be instantly devoured. The skit was fresh and funny *and* old.

Aesop told the same basic story in fable form in the sixth century B.C. Rather than land sharks or proselytizers Aesop told of a wolf pretending to be the mother of a young goat locked behind its door. The Brothers Grimm published the first dramatic or folktale version, "The Wolf and the Seven Little Kids," in 1812. In the 25 centuries since Aesop, the tale has changed and grown in many ways while staying the same. In the last 150 years alone it has been collected throughout Europe, Asia, Africa, India, and sections of the Americas. The range of narrative twists is wide, as is the variety of tones. Yet all remain the same: Aesop, Grimm, *Saturday Night Live,* and the flyer at the local supermarket.

Scope

A Knock at the Door is an exploration and celebration of these differences and the ultimate unity they reveal. It was compiled for all who enjoy stories—children *and* adults—as well as parents, teachers, librarians, and storytellers who love to share tales. The range of plot twists and images in these tales is at times extreme. While anyone old enough to read them is most likely ready for these tales, not all of them are as appropriate for sharing with younger children as is the best-known version "The Wolf and the Seven Little Kids." For example, third grade children could read or hear and enjoy "The Story of Demane and Demazana" and "The Lame Wolf," but stories such as "Journey to the Mending City" and "Indesoka," which feature violent villains and human children, not animals, may be too intense and should be shared with older children from fifth grade up. Selection and discretion are important, but so is acknowledging the wide range of the tale's versions. In honoring all variants, those who experience them will discover the tales and their tellers are united not in spite of their cultural differences, but *through* them. Difference as well as the knock at the door becomes a common bond.

In their classic reference work, *The Types of the Folktale,* Antti Aarne and Stith Thompson classified a large number of tale types or story plots found in the world. They have classified the basic story featured in all "knock at the door" tales as Tale Type 123 or "The Wolf and the Kids: The wolf comes in the absence of the mother and eats up the kids" (Aarne, 1928, 33). The innate mutability of tales and the subjectiveness involved in folklore have brought a somewhat nebulous group of tales to be identified as type 123. Some people have included any tale in which a villain knocks on a door and/or breaks down the door. By this definition "The Three Little Pigs" (British) would qualify. Other tales such as "Budulinek" (Czech) in which the wolf seduces the boy into opening the door for a ride on his tail have also been ascribed to type 123. Even tales in which the children meet with the villain while out walking where they have been told not to go, such as "The Disobedient Little Rabbits" (Taos/Native American) have been classified as matching the other tales.

I have kept a more narrow focus for this collection by including only tales that involve a dangerous character knocking at the door and pretending to be a familiar, protective family member or friend. Hundreds of variants have been collected over the years. Of those available in English, I have selected 34 tales from 33 cultures. A thirty-fifth tale in Spanish is included from Mexico. Notes for the tales include citations for more than 40 additional variants.

Arrangement

Because all 35 tales have the same primary theme or story I have loosely arranged them in the manner of Aaron Copland's *Appalachian Spring:* Beginning with Aesop's fable each additional tale shares a more developed and expansive variation of the initial theme while gaining resonance from the tales around it.

Following the Tales section is the Tale Notes section, which lists each tale's source or sources. If available, the note gives the date and place and manner in which the tale was collected. Equally important is the brief contextual information about each tale. Though many anthologies would have readers believe so, no folktale exists in a vacuum. Being aware of a tale's cultural environment places the tale and the telling in the ongoing flow of stories and people. More resources follow the tale notes.

The Essays section begins with "One Tale Around the World," which is a comparative overview of all the tales included in this book. "A Telling Look at Pictures" examines the many ways "The Wolf and the Seven Little Kids" has been illustrated and what these artists have to offer the storyteller. "Telling with the Current: Helping Children and Folktales Teach Themselves" explores ways the teacher or librarian and teller can develop a greater awareness of a tale's cultural context within the audience. "A Door with Many Windows" is a bibliographic essay of materials offering psychological, social, and legal interpretations of "The Wolf and the Seven Little Kids." A bibliography of reference sources concludes the book.

Sharing the Stories

As Anne Pellowski so beautifully shares in *The World of Storytelling* (1977, 1990), styles and occasions of storytelling vary throughout the world. Difference again is a common bond. Honoring these differences is important, but honoring is different than mimicking. Simply trying to copy a tale's culture can begin to distract and diminish what the tale has to share. As the characters in these tales come to learn, sound and image (e.g., accent and costume) do not ensure nurturance, truth, or the "real thing." Far more important than costumes or "show and tell" souvenirs is the teller's belief in the tale's essential *story*. This does not mean believing in talking animals and magic, but a belief in what the story is about or the emotional experience at the heart of the tale. It is the emotional experience the teller needs to evoke within the listener to bring the story to life.

In the case of this collection it is a shared essential story: The fear and exhilaration of being left home alone for the first time. Knowing you've done your best and still getting duped. Pretending to be someone else—no matter how briefly—to gain something. Discovering someone you trusted was actually working against you. The absolute terror of someone bursting into your protected area. Hiding from impending danger. Returning to find your home destroyed. The grief of losing loved ones. Feeling yourself completely overwhelmed, then finding some reborn part of yourself that is ready to try again. The essential story of *A Knock at the Door* is all of these, plus each teller's and listener's personal fascination and connection with the tale.

By definition variants of a tale share the same essential story, but the overriding emotional tone of a specific variant may be quite different from the next. A change in key from major to minor or a change in tempo not only changes the song, it changes what is shared. The same is true of folktales. Within this collection the tone of tales varies from the comic touch of "The Goat, the Kids, and the Wolf" (French) to the dark and horrific world of "Indesoka" (Malagasy). Romance frames the Haitian variant "La

Belle Venus," while righteous revenge fills "The Cunning Snake" (African-American). Time and again tales are different while being the same.

No matter which variant or variants one shares, those listening may take the teller to be the wolf at *their* door. The story is familiar, but the voice or words are wrong. Listeners may deem both the teller and tale to be false and send them away. Simply being honest will circumvent most conflicts of this nature. Acknowledge the listeners' memories of the tale type (most likely "The Wolf and the Seven Little Kids") as *one* good way to tell the story. Referring to the "new" variant as a different way to tell the story and briefly discussing how folktales change can help establish a sense of coexistence between tales and cultures rather than one of threatened replacement.

The tales included here have all been distilled and intensified through years of infinite tellings. They have become what Gaston Bachelard calls "reserves of enthusiasm which help us believe in the world, love the world, create our world. . . . Each archetype is an opening on the world, an invitation to the world" (Bachelard, 1971, 124). May they be read and shared with such joy in mind.

I have wanted to retell "The Wolf and the Seven Little Kids" for many years. It has entertained, puzzled, and comforted me since childhood. And, in the end, it even helped me survive this project. Now I not only get to retell it but share it shot through a prism in all its cultural and emotional colors.

Acknowledgments

A collection like this is never done alone. Without the field work of others over the last 150 years this book could not exist. And taking advantage of those sources would be impossible without the vital support of libraries. I especially want to thank the Kerlan Collection at the University of Minnesota and Kay Henning—Queen of Interlibrary Loan—at the University of Wisconsin-Eau Claire.

Most of all I give special thanks to Beatrice Sweet for her wisdom and patience and to David Holter for his love and support.

Acknowledgments to Contributors

Grateful acknowledgment is made to the following for permission to reprint their copyrighted material. Every reasonable effort has been made to trace the ownership of all copyrighted stories in this volume. Any errors that may have occurred are inadvertent and will be corrected in subsequent editions, provided notification is sent to the publisher. Stories not listed are assumed to be in the public domain.

Martha Warren Beckwith. "Tiger Softens His Voice" from *Jamaica Anansi Stories.* Memoirs of American Folk-Lore Society. Volume 15. Part 1 by Martha Warren Beckwith, copyright © 1924 by American Folk-Lore Society. Reproduced by permission of the American Folk-Lore Society, Memoirs of the American Folk-Lore Society, Volume 15, Part 1, 1924. Not for further reproduction.

Margaret Wise Brown. "The Wolf and the Kid" from *The Fables of La Fontaine* translated by Margaret Wise Brown, copyright © 1940 by Harper and Brothers. Reprinted by permission of HarperCollins.

Cora Cheney. "The Tiger Witch" from *Tales from a Taiwan Kitchen* by Cora Cheney, copyright © 1976 by Cora Cheney. Reprinted by permission of G.P. Putnam's Sons.

Charles Coxwell. "The Goat and the Kids" from *Siberian and Other Folk Tales: Primitive Literature of the Empire of the Tsar* collected and translated by Charles Fillingham Coxwell, copyright © 1925 by C.W. Daniel Publishers. Reprinted by permission of C.W. Daniel Publishers, 1 Church Path, Saffron Walden, Essex CB10 1JP England.

Kamini Dinesh. "The Lame Wolf" from *Folk Tales of Rajasthan* retold by Kamini Dinesh, copyright © 1979 by Kamini Dinesh. Reprinted by permission of Jainsons and Jain Brothers.

Geraldine Elliot. "The Monkey and the Hyena" from *The Long Grass Whispers* by Geraldine Elliot, copyright © 1939 by Geraldine Elliot. Reprinted by permission of Watkins, Loomis Agency, Inc.

Edith Fowke. "A Granny Who Had Many Children" from *Folk Lore of Canada* collected by Edith Fowke, copyright © 1976 by McClelland and Stewart. Used by permission of the Canadian publishers, McClelland and Stewart, Toronto.

Gyneth Johnson. "La Belle Venus" from *How Donkeys Came to Haiti and Other Tales* retold by Gyneth Johnson, copyright © 1949 by Devin-Adair, Publishers, Old Greenwich, Connecticut, 06870. Permission granted to reprint "La Belle Venus" by Gyneth Johnson, 1949. All rights reserved. Reprinted by permission of Devin-Adair.

Ernest Balintuma Kalibala. "The Grandmother and the Apes" from *Wakaima and the Clay Man and Other African Folk Tales* by Ernest Balintuma Kalibala and Mary Gould Davis, copyright © 1946 by Longmans Green and Co. Reprinted by permission of Random House, Inc.

Genevieve Massignon. "The Goat, the Kids, and the Wolf" from *Folktales from France* edited by Genevieve Massignon and translated by Jacqueline Hyland, copyright © 1968 by University of Chicago Press. Reprinted by permission of University of Chicago Press.

Ibrahim Muhawi. "The Little She-Goat" from *Speak, Bird, Speak Again: Palestinian Arab Folktales* edited by Ibrahim Muhawi and Sharif Kanaana, copyright © 1988 by The Regents of the University of California. Reprinted by permission of University of California Press.

Elsie Clews Parsons. "The Devil Hammers His Tongue" from *Folk-Lore of the Antilles, English and French.* (Memoirs of the American Folk-Lore Society. Volume 26. Part 1) by Elsie Clews Parsons, copyright © 1933 by the American Folk-Lore Society. Reproduced by permission of the American Folk-Lore Society from Memoirs of the American Folk-Lore Society, Volume 26, Part 1. Not for sale or further reproduction.

———. "The Three Kids" from *Folk-Lore from the Cape Verde Islands.* (Memoirs of the American Folk-Lore Society. Volume 15. Part 1) by Elsie Clews Parsons, copyright © 1923 by the American Folk-Lore Society. Reproduced by permission of the American Folk-Lore Society from Memoirs of the American Folk-Lore Society, Volume 15, Part 1, 1923. Not for further reproduction.

Stanley L. Robe. "Los Seis Cabritos" from *Mexican Tales and Legends from Los Altos* by Stanley L. Robe, copyright © 1970 by University of California Press. Reprinted by permission of University of California Press.

Yona Sabar. "The Ewe, the Goat, and the Lion" from *The Folk Literature of the Kurdistani Jews: An Anthology* translated from Hebrew and Neo-Aramic by Yona Sabar, copyright © 1982 by Yale University Press. Reprinted by permission of Yale University Press.

Keigo Seki. "The Golden Chain from Heaven" from *Folktales of Japan* edited by Keigo Seki and translated by Robert J. Adams, copyright © 1963 by University of Chicago Press. Reprinted by permission of University of Chicago Press.

Loreto Todd. "When a Wise Man Dies, a Wise Man Buries Him" from *Some Day Been Day: West African Pidgin Folktales* by Loreto Todd, copyright © 1979 by Loreto Todd. Reprinted by permission of Tortoise Books.

"The Wolf and the Goat" from *Russian Fairy Tales* by Aleksandr Afanas'ev translated by Norbert Guterman, copyright © 1945 by Pantheon Books, Inc. and renewed 1973 by Random House, Inc. Reprinted by permission of Pantheon Books, a division of Random House, Inc.

"The Wolf and the Seven Little Kids" from *The Complete Grimms' Fairy Tales* by Jacob Karl Ludwig and Wilhelm Karl Grimm, translated by Margaret Hunt, copyright © 1944 by Pantheon Books, Inc. and renewed 1972 by Random House, Inc. Reprinted by permission of Pantheon Books, a division of Random House, Inc.

Zong In-Sob. "The Sun and the Moon" from *Folk Tales from Korea* by Zong In-Sob, copyright © 1952 by Routledge and Kegan Paul. Reprinted by permission of Grove Press.

The Tales

The Kid and the Wolf

Many people believe this to be the oldest version of the "knock at the door" type of story. It was created by Aesop and told in the oral tradition for centuries before it was ever written down. Aesop, a former slave, lived in Thrace, an area of Greece, during the sixth century B.C. You may know some of his other fables such as "The Tortoise and the Hare" and "The Dog and the Bone." This early version in fable form is only the first half of later, longer versions.

A mother goat in need of food went out and left her kid at home. Before she left she told him to keep the door locked and not open it for anyone till she returned. The wolf who was lurking near by heard the mother's orders. Once she was gone the wolf knocked on the door and called out in the mother's voice saying he needed in. The kid looked through the crack in the door and saw it was the wolf and not his mother. He refused to open the door and said, "Go away. You may call out in my mother's voice, but you're only a fake. You want to break in and eat me."

The Kid and the Wolf

The Wolf, the Goat and the Kid

*J*ean de la Fontaine of France based his story on Aesop's fable. It was one of many he wrote between 1668 and 1694. Children in France know La Fontaine's fables as well as children in the United States know tales like "The Three Little Pigs." This tale is told in fable form and ends with a moral, which is meant to tell people what they should learn from the story. Some fables can have several different morals.

*O*ne day the nanny goat longed for the greener fields far from home. She locked the door of her house. But before she left she said to her kid, "Guard yourself well, my little one, and for your life's sake don't open the door to anyone unless they let you know who they are by saying these words: 'Down with the wolf and all his race!' That is the watchword of goats."

But even as she was telling her kid these words the wolf happened to pass by. He heard what she said and kept the words in his memory for further use. The little kid closed the door without catching sight of the hungry wolf.

As soon as the wolf saw that the nanny goat was out of sight he made his voice high and goatish and went to the door and demanded in a hypocritical, sweet voice, "Little kid, little kid, open the door! Down with the wolf! Quick, open the door!"

The wolf thought the kid would open right away. But the kid was wary. He pushed through a crack in the door and said, "Show me your white paw, or I will never open this door."

Now, as everyone knows, white paws do not grow on wolves. And the wolf, surprised at such words from a little kid, went back to where he came from.

And where would the little kid be now if he had depended on a watchword which any passing wolf might overhear? Two precautions are better than one, and more than two are never wasted.

Four Disobedient Kids

This tale was retold by a woman named Bozena Nemcova around the year 1850. She lived in the area of Europe known as Southern Bohemia, which is now called Czechoslovakia. One of the reasons she wrote it was to express pride in her local culture, something that had long been forbidden by invading authorities. In this version the villain at the door is a fox. It features four kids instead of just one and has a unique ending.

*O*nce upon a time there lived a mother goat with four little kids. One day she had to go away, but before she left she warned her children, "When I leave I'll shut the door tight. But no matter what, no matter who knocks, do not open the door till you hear my voice."

The four kids promised to keep the door closed and the mother felt safe in going away. But before she had been gone very long Fox came by and called to the kids.

"My dear little kids. Open up. It's mother. I've got fresh milk for you."

The four kids listened and shook their heads.

"No," they said. "Your voice is not our mother's voice. Hers is much thinner than yours."

Fox ran away, but not for long. This time when he knocked and called his voice was much thinner than the time before.

"My dear little kids. Open up. It's mother. I've got fresh milk for you."

The kids listened and shook their heads no. "Your voice is not our mother's voice. Hers is still much thinner than yours."

Fox ran away, but not for long. This time when he knocked he called out in the thinnest voice he could make.

"My dear little kids. Open up. It's mother. I've got fresh milk for you."

This time the kids couldn't be sure. One said it was their mother's voice. Another said it wasn't. A third said it was. The fourth said it wasn't.

When they couldn't agree they began to fight. In moments they were fighting so hard they knocked open the door themselves. And before they had time to close it again Fox jumped in and swallowed them all.

Four Disobedient Kids

The Goat and the Kids

*T*his tale was told by a group of people called Mordvins. They live in a section of Russia, a country that used to be part of the Soviet Union. Though this version is still very brief, it begins to explore the question of what might happen if the wolf is successful in tricking the kids into opening the door. The various answers to this question create the last half of the story in longer versions.

A goat lived in the forest with her kids; she used to shut them in a mud hut whenever she went into the forest. There she ate and drank; then, on returning home, she would sing near the hut in a gentle voice, "Little kids, sucklings, open and come out. I, your mother have been in the forest and eaten grass, I have drunk water from the brook; milk gathers in my udder, from my udder it flows on to my hoof, from my hoof into a little hollow and from the little hollow onto the ground."

The kids came out, partook of the milk and went back. The goat shut them up and said, "Mind, do not open, do not let a wolf deceive you!" "We will not open, little mother!" The goat returned into the forest, and a wolf heard her singing. He came near and began to sing like the goat, but in a rough voice; "Little kids, sucklings, come out, open! I am your mother, I have been to the forest." But the kids called out to him, "You are deceiving us, your voice is not like our mother's; her voice is fine and beautiful, but yours is rough and disagreeable."

The wolf went away dissatisfied. He was angry and sharpened his tongue on a whetstone; then coming back to the kids, he began to sing in a delicate voice, "Little kids, my sucklings, come out, open! I am your mother, I have been for a walk in the forest, and eaten various kinds of grass, I drank water from a rivulet; milk is gathering in my udder, from my udder it flows on to one of my hoofs, from my hoof into a little hollow, and from the little hollow on to the ground."

The kids thought the visitor was their mother and, opening the door, they frisked out. The wolf strangled them. The goat arrived and sang again and again, but the kids did not come. She guessed correctly that the wolf had killed them and she sobbed. Then she left the forest and went to live in a village; there she now dwells with her owner.

The Goat and the Kids

The Devil Hammers His Tongue

*A*n American woman named Elsie Clews Parsons collected this story from a 13-year-old boy living in St. George, Grenada, in the Caribbean Sea. In this version the villain is a devil and the mother is a person. But, unlike most mothers in these tales, this one does not love all her children equally. This version is told in the different kind of English, or *dialect*, that people in Grenada speak.

A woman she had three children, one name' Minnie, one name' Minnie Batania, the other name' Crocodile. The mother didn't like Crocodile at all. Every time when she goes to town she used to buy sweets and she used to sing,

> *Minnie Batania*
> *Come here!*
> *Minnie Po,*
> *Come here!*
> *Minnie Batania come here.*
> *And let Crocodile stop there.*

One day the devil heard her singing it and he came and said,

> *Minnie Batania,*
> *Come here!*
> *Minnie Po,*
> *Come here!*
> *Minnie Batania come here,*
> *And let Crocodile stop there.*

[in gruff voice]

The children say, "That's not mother's voice." He went to the blacksmith shop and he beat his tongue upon the anvil and he came back again and he began to sing,

> *Minnie Batania,*
> *Come here!*
> *Minnie Po,*
> *Come here!*
> *Minnie Batania come here,*
> *And let Crocodile stop there.*

[in gentle voice]

Then the children come. And he ate them all up, excepting to Crocodile. And when the mother came she began to sing,

> *Minnie Batania,*
> *Come here!*
> *Minnie Po,*
> *Come here!*
> *Minnie Batania come here,*
> *And let Crocodile stop there.*

And Crocodile reply

> *Minnie Minnie not there,*
> *Minnie Po not there,*
> *Minnie Batania not there,*
> *And me Crocodile that's here.*

And the mother gave all the sweets and cake to Crocodile. And she liked Crocodile until she died.

The Story of the Wolf and the Goat

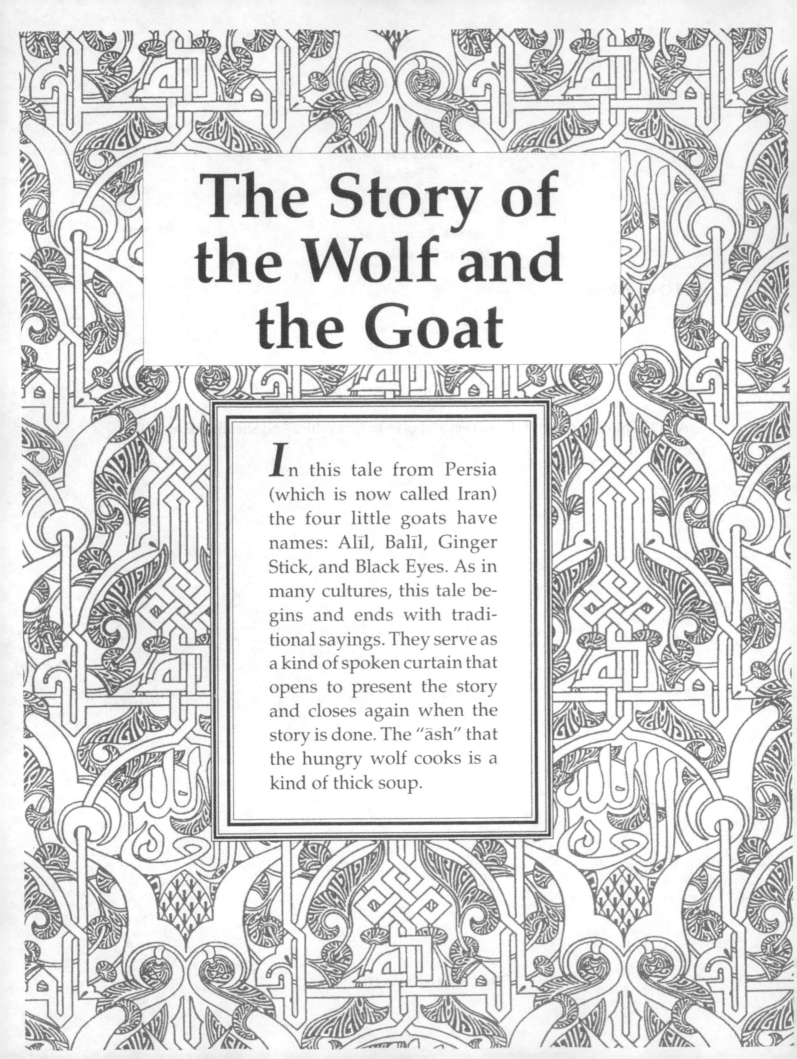

*I*n this tale from Persia (which is now called Iran) the four little goats have names: Alīl, Balīl, Ginger Stick, and Black Eyes. As in many cultures, this tale begins and ends with traditional sayings. They serve as a kind of spoken curtain that opens to present the story and closes again when the story is done. The "āsh" that the hungry wolf cooks is a kind of thick soup.

*O*nce upon a time there was a time
when there was no one but
GOD.

There was a goat who had four children, one was Alīl, one was Balīl, one was Ginger Stick, and the fourth was Black Eyes.

One day she said: "Sit quietly here, children; I'm going off to bring grass for you. If the wolf should come and knock, don't open the door for him. And if he says: 'I am your mother,' say: 'Put your hand in at the crack of the door,' and if you see that the hand is black, don't open the door, but if you see a red hand you'll know that it's your mother back again."

Now the wolf had all the time been listening, and as soon as the goat was gone he dyed his hand with henna to make it red, and came and knocked at the door. They called out: "Who's that?"

"Open the door, I've brought grass for you," said he. "Show us your hand." The wolf shoved his hand in at the crack of the door, and when they saw that it was red they opened the door and let him in. So he carried off Alīl and Balīl and Ginger Stick, but Black Eyes ran away and hid.

When the mother goat came back she saw there was no one in the house and she began to call. Then Black Eyes came out of his hiding-place and told his mother how the wolf had carried off his brothers. So they went together and climbed on to the roof of the wolf's house. They saw that he was just cooking some *āsh*, and they threw down a handful of earth into it.

The wolf cried:

> *Who are you on my roof up there?*
> *You dare to throw earth in my āsh, you dare?*
> *My āsh all salty and bad you've made,*
> *My eyes all blind and sad you've made.*

Then answered the goat:

The goat, the goat so fleet am I,
The goat with bells on her feet am I.
I can dance with my feet so fleet,
Leaping about on my hinder-feet.
You have stolen Alīl of mine,
You have stolen Balīl of mine,
You have stolen my Ginger Stick.

And the wolf said: "Yes, I've stolen them"; and the goat said: "Come, let's go and fight."

The goat went and got a skin and filled it full of curds and butter to make a nice present, and carried it off to the knife-grinder and said: "Come along and sharpen my horns."

The wolf went and got a skin too, but he was too stingy to put in butter or anything nice, so he blew it up with wind till it looked very full indeed, and took it for a gift to a man who was a tooth-puller, and he said: "Come along and sharpen my teeth." The dentist wondered what his present was, and opened the top of the skin a little to peep in and see, but behold, there was only wind inside! And the air ran out puff, puff, puff.

He said nothing at all, but instead of sharpening the wolf's teeth he pulled them all out, and in the holes he put little pointed twists of cotton-wool that looked like nice sharp, white teeth.

Then up came the goat and they went off to fight. First they came to a little stream of water. The goat said: "Come, let's first drink our fill," and she put her head down over the water, but she took care to drink none herself. The wolf drank and drank till he could drink no more.

Then the goat said: "Come along, let's jump across the stream," and with that she leaped over neatly. The wolf went to jump over too, but he was so swollen up with water that he fell in. Then the goat smote him in the stomach with one of her sharp horns and tore it right open, and so he died.

And off she carried Alīl and Balīl and Ginger Stick, and brought them home again to Black Eyes.

And now my story has come to an end,
but the sparrow never got
home.

The Wolf and the Goat

*T*his tale is very popular in Russia, one country that was part of the former Soviet Union. It was first published for a wide audience in 1866 by the lawyer Aleksandr Afanas'ev. Life in peasant Russia often centered around the warmth of the stove's fire. Fire also plays a vital role in how the mother goat saves her kids in this version *and* how she gets even with the gluttonous wolf.

*O*nce upon a time there was a goat who built herself a little hut in the woods and lived there with her kids. She often went deep into the forest to look for food; whenever she left the hut the kids locked the little door and stayed inside. When the goat returned she would knock at the door and sing: "My little baby kids, unlock the door and open it! I, the she-goat, have been in the forest; I have eaten soft grass and drunk spring water. Milk flows down in the udder and from the udder to the hoof and from the hoof into the damp earth." The kids would at once open the door and let their mother in. Then she would feed them and go again into the forest, and the kids would lock the door very tight.

The wolf overhead all this. Once when the goat had gone to the forest he came to the little hut and cried in his rough voice: "Hey, little kids, hey my dear ones, unlock the door and open it! Your mother is back and has brought you milk aplenty." But the kids answered: "We hear you, we hear you, but yours is not our mother's voice! Our mother sings in a soft voice and sings different words." The wolf went away and hid himself. Then the goat came and knocked at the door, singing: "My little baby kids, unlock the door and open it! I, the she-goat, have been in the forest, I have eaten soft grass and drunk spring water. Milk flows down in the udder and from the udder to the hoof and from the hoof into the damp earth." The kids let their mother in and told her that the wolf had come and tried to devour them. The goat fed them and when she left again for the woods gave them strict orders not to let in anyone who might come to the little hut and beg in a rough voice saying other words than she said. As soon as the goat was gone the wolf ran to the little hut, knocked at the door, and began to chant in a soft voice: "My little baby kids, unlock the door and open it! I, the she-goat, have been in the forest, I have eaten soft grass and drunk spring water. Milk flows down in the udder to the hoof and from the hoof into the damp earth." The kids opened the door and the wolf ran in and ate them all; only one little kid escaped by hiding in the stove.

The goat came back, but no matter how sweetly she sang, no one answered her. She came closer to the door and saw that it was open; she looked into the room and saw that it was empty; she looked into the stove and found one kid there.

When the goat learned of her misfortune, she sat down on a bench, began to weep bitterly, and sang: "Oh, my baby kids, why did you open the door to the wicked wolf? He has devoured you all, and left me with great grief and sadness in my soul." The wolf heard this, came into the hut, and said to the goat: "Ah, neighbor, neighbor, why do you

The Wolf and the Goat

slander me? Would I do such a thing? Let us go to the forest together and take a walk." "No, neighbor, I have no heart for walking." "Let us go," the wolf insisted.

They went into the forest and found a pit in which some brigands had recently cooked gruel. There was still some fire left in it. The goat said to the wolf: "Neighbor, let us see which of us can jump across the pit." The wolf tried first, and fell into the hot pit; his belly burst from the heat of the fire, and the kids ran out of it and rushed to their mother. From then on they lived happily, acquired wisdom, and eschewed evil.

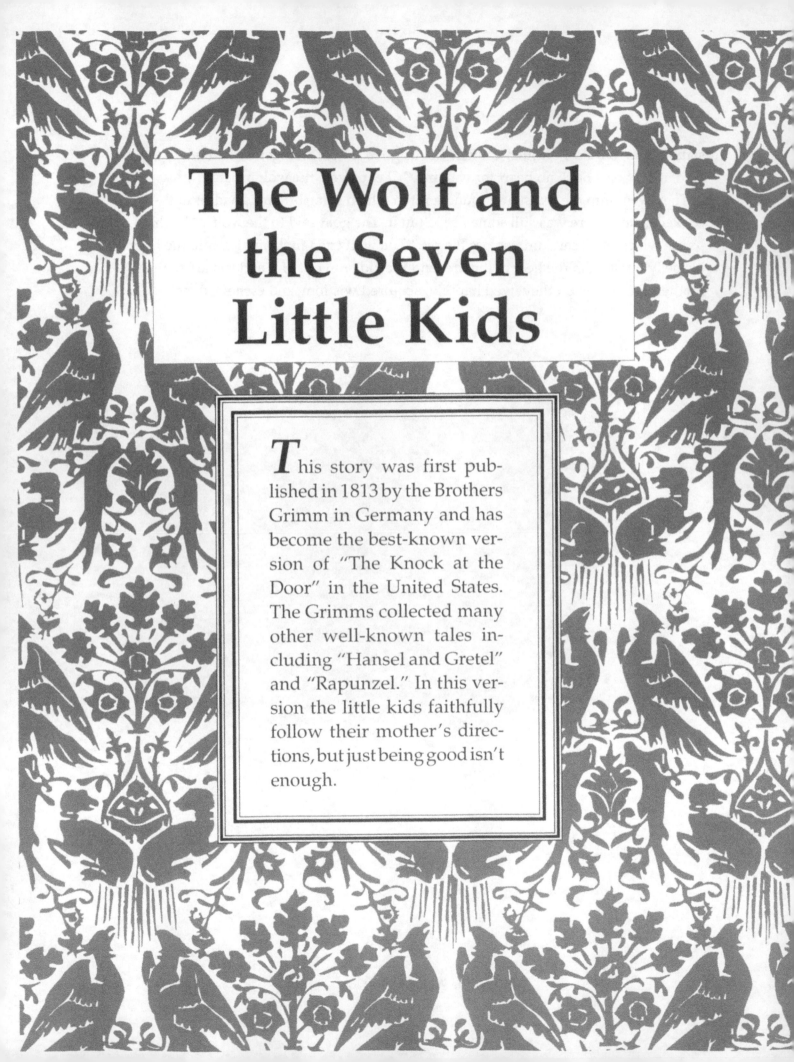

The Wolf and the Seven Little Kids

*T*his story was first published in 1813 by the Brothers Grimm in Germany and has become the best-known version of "The Knock at the Door" in the United States. The Grimms collected many other well-known tales including "Hansel and Gretel" and "Rapunzel." In this version the little kids faithfully follow their mother's directions, but just being good isn't enough.

*T*here was once upon a time an old goat who had seven little kids, and loved them with all the love of a mother for her children. One day she wanted to go into the forest and fetch some food. So she called all seven to her and said: "Dear children, I have to go into the forest, be on your guard against the wolf; if he comes in, he will devour you all—skin, hair, and everything. The wretch often disguises himself, but you will know him at once by his rough voice and his black feet." The kids said: "Dear mother, we will take good care of ourselves; you may go away without any anxiety." Then the old one bleated, and went on her way with an easy mind.

It was not long before some one knocked at the house-door and called: "Open the door, dear children; your mother is here, and has brought something back with her for each of you." But the little kids knew that it was the wolf, by the rough voice. "We will not open the door," cried they, "you are not our mother. She has a soft, pleasant voice, but your voice is rough; you are the wolf!" Then the wolf went away to a shopkeeper and bought himself a great lump of chalk, ate this and made his voice soft with it. Then he came back, knocked at the door of the house, and called: "Open the door, dear children, your mother is here and has brought something back with her for each of you." But the wolf had laid his black paws against the window, and the children saw them and cried: "We will not open the door, our mother has not black feet like you: you are the wolf!" Then the wolf ran to a baker and said: "I have hurt my feet, rub some dough over them for me." And when the baker had rubbed his feet over, he ran to the miller and said: "Strew some white meal over my feet for me." The miller thought to himself: "The wolf wants to deceive someone," and refused; but the wolf said: "If you will not do it, I will devour you." Then the miller was afraid, and made his paws white for him. Truly, this is the way of mankind.

So now the wretch went for the third time to the house-door, knocked at it and said: "Open the door for me, children, your dear little mother has come home, and has brought every one of you something back from the forest with her." The little kids cried: "First show us your paws that we may know if you are our dear little mother." Then he put his paws in through the window, and when the kids saw that they were white, they believed that all he said was true, and opened the door. But who should come in but the wolf! They were terrified and wanted to hide themselves. One sprang under the table, the second into the bed, the third into the stove, the fourth into the kitchen, the fifth into the cupboard, the sixth under the washing-bowl, and the seventh into the clock-case. But the wolf found them all, and used no great ceremony; one after the other he swallowed them down his throat. The youngest, who was in the clock-case, was the only one he did not find. When the wolf had satisfied his appetite he took himself off, laid himself down under a tree in the green meadow outside, and began to sleep. Soon afterwards the old goat came home again from the forest. Ah! what a sight she saw there! The house-door stood wide open. The table, chairs, and benches were thrown down, the washing-bowl lay broken to pieces, and the quilts and pillows were pulled off the bed. She sought her children, but they were nowhere to be found. She called them one after another by name, but no one answered. At last, when she came to the youngest, a soft voice cried: "Dear mother, I am in the clock-case." She took the kid out, and it told her that the wolf had come and had eaten all the others. Then you may imagine how she wept over her poor children.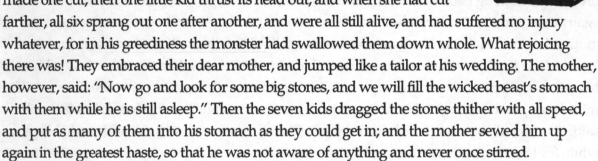

At length in her grief she went out, and the youngest kid ran with her. When they came to the meadow, there lay the wolf by the tree and snored so loud that the branches shook. She looked at him on every side and saw that something was moving and struggling in his gorged belly. "Ah, heavens," she said, "is it possible that my poor children whom he has swallowed down for his supper, can be still alive?" Then the kid had to run home and fetch scissors, and a needle and thread, and the goat cut open the monster's stomach, and hardly had she made one cut, then one little kid thrust its head out, and when she had cut farther, all six sprang out one after another, and were all still alive, and had suffered no injury whatever, for in his greediness the monster had swallowed them down whole. What rejoicing there was! They embraced their dear mother, and jumped like a tailor at his wedding. The mother, however, said: "Now go and look for some big stones, and we will fill the wicked beast's stomach with them while he is still asleep." Then the seven kids dragged the stones thither with all speed, and put as many of them into his stomach as they could get in; and the mother sewed him up again in the greatest haste, so that he was not aware of anything and never once stirred.

When the wolf at length had had his fill of sleep, he got on his legs, and as the stones in his stomach made him very thirsty, he wanted to go to a well to drink. But when he began to walk and to move about the stones in his stomach knocked against each other and rattled. Then cried he:

> *What rumbles and tumbles*
> *Against my poor bones?*
> *I thought 'twas six kids,*
> *But it feels like big stones.*

And when he got to the well and stooped over the water to drink, the heavy stones made him fall in, and he had to drown miserably. When the seven kids saw that, they came running to the spot and cried aloud: "The wolf is dead! The wolf is dead!" and danced for joy round about the well with their mother.

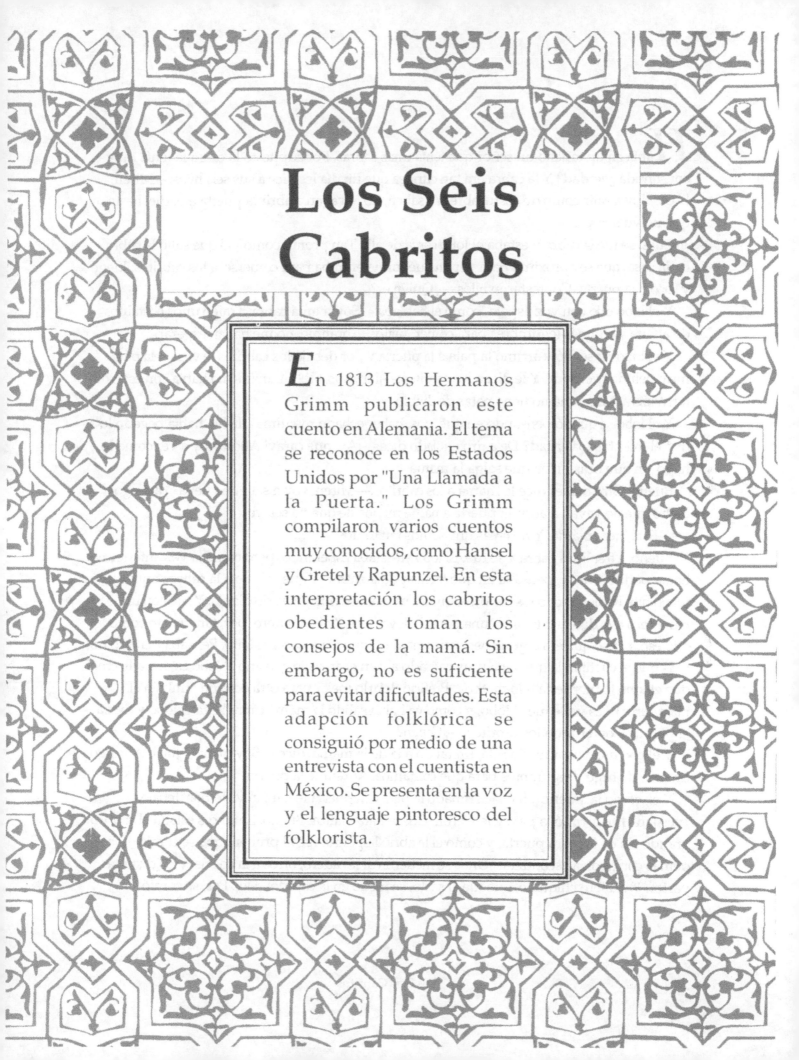

Los Seis Cabritos

*E*n 1813 Los Hermanos Grimm publicaron este cuento en Alemania. El tema se reconoce en los Estados Unidos por "Una Llamada a la Puerta." Los Grimm compilaron varios cuentos muy conocidos, como Hansel y Gretel y Rapunzel. En esta interpretación los cabritos obedientes toman los consejos de la mamá. Sin embargo, no es suficiente para evitar dificultades. Esta adapción folklórica se consiguió por medio de una entrevista con el cuentista en México. Se presenta en la voz y el lenguaje pintoresco del folklorista.

*H*abía en un rancho un señor que tenía unas cabras. Por supuesto la cabra la tenía muy consentida ¿verdad? Y la cabra era tan curiosa que un día les dice a sus seis hijos:—Miren, hijos. Voy a salir como de costumbre. Ya saben, no le vayan a abrir la puerta a nadie hasta que no vuelva yo.

Pues, se fue la cabra y estaba el lobo cerca de allí. Tan pronto como vió que salió la cabra de la casa, que se aproximó para ver en qué forma entraba para comerse a los cabritos. Llegó y tocó a la puerta. Contestaron ellos:—¿Quién es?

Y el lobo dijo con voz áspera, como él hablaba:—Soy mamá cabra. Traigo unos costalitos de alfalfa y algunas legumbres para comer, hijitos. Ábranme, no me hagan esperar.

Y el lobo no se fijó y arrimó la pata a la puerta y por debajo los cabritos le vieron la pata muy peluda ¿verdad?. Y le dicen los cabritos:—¡No, hombre! Mi mamá no habla con esa voz tan áspera. Mi mamá no tiene patas de diablo.

Y el lobo se quedó pensando en que, pos, haber echado mentiras allí. No había pegado lo que él intentaba ¿verdad? De a tiro enojado dice:—¡Ay, qué caray! Ahora voy a ver cómo lo hago, en otra ocasión en que salga la mamá.

Bueno. Otro día les dice la mamá a los cabritos:—Miren, voy a salir de vuelta. Ya tengo dicho que no vayan a abrir la puerta a nadie menos de que no sea yo.

—Está bien, mamá. Y no creas que somos tan tontos.

Bueno. Ya salió la cabra y se fue. El lobo ya estaba esperando, pero como la vez anterior no había podido entrar, pensaba en qué forma podía entrar. Y que le vino a la cabeza aquel relajo que habían dicho los cabritos, que su mamá no tenía patas de diablo. Y fue con un panadero y le dijo que le diera una poca de levadura. Y el panadero, pos, tan pronto como le dijo eso, pensó que era alguna hechuría (maldad) que iba a hacer el lobo. Pensaba matarlo no más que el cuchillo le quedaba muy retirado allí en el amasijo, y como el lobo estaba allí, creó que el lobo lo mordería o lo mataría. Prefirió dejarlo mejor para otra ocasión también el panadero. Pues ya se fue el lobo, y como ya había salido la mamá cabra llega el lobo y toca a la puerta. Contestaron los cabritos:—¿Quién?

Y él con una voz muy fingida, imitando a la de la mamá, dice:—Soy mamá, que hoy traigo un saco de trigo y legumbres para que comamos. Ábranme la puerta.

Y él, como la anterior, había arrimado la pata a la puerta le habían visto por debajo, ¿verdad? Pos arrimó la pata y le vieron ellos la pata blanca. Bueno. Entonces estaba el cabrito grande allí en la mera puerta, y como él le abrió la puerta fue el primero que se comió. Los demás corrieron a esconderse. Unos se metieron al lavadero, otros a la cocina, y en distintas partes. Y el mero chiquillo, que fue el sexto, se metió en la caja del reloj. Pos, se comió

Los Seis Cabritos

aquellos cinco y como no encontró nada más se llenó. Ya se fue a dormir al pie de un árbol cerca de la casa.

Pos, cuando vuelve la mamá, ve la puerta abrierta, ve todo en desorden, todos los muebles, todo lo que tenían allí voltiado, y que se asusta ella y lamentando, comienza a gritar que dónde están sus hijitos. Pues muy horrorizada ella, muy triste, pues, por la falta de sus hijos. Pero allá responde el más chiquillo que estaba en la caja del reloj:—Acá estoy yo.

Y ya fue ella y con trabajo lo sacó de la caja del reloj y le preguntó que dónde estaban los demás. Dice:—Pos vino el lobo y se los comió.

—Hijo, pos ¿a dónde se fue el lobo?, dice.

—Pos, el lobo está por áhi cerca. Yo creo que ha de estar por áhi en el árbol.

La mamá llorando y como quiera dijo:—¡Hombre! ¡Traíte el cuchillo!

Muy enojada, salió ella y el cabrito, ¿verdad?, a ver donde estaba el lobo. Llegaron y estaba el lobo al pie del árbol que estaba áhi cerca de la casa. Y estaba dormido, como estaba él muy lleno. Y fue la mamá de los cabritos y con el cuchillo le rompió la panza y fue sacando de uno por uno los cabritos, y cuál fue su sorpresa que todavía estaban vivos ellos. Ya que sacó el último entonces cosió la panza del lobo pero antes de coserla le metió unas piedras. Le llenó el estómago de piedras al lobo. Pues, el lobo siguió dormido. No sintió nada.

Ya se vino la mamá acá con todos sus hijitos, recontenta y los cabritos detrás de ella cantando y se elogiaban de aquel triunfo que habían tenido, que le habían ganado al lobo. Esa vez comienza el lobo, despierta con mucha sed y oye la canción y la algarabía que tenían allá los cabritos y la mamá, y le llama le atención, pues, de que él había comido los cinco cabritos, hijos de la cabra. Y se fue a buscar el tanque que estaba cerca de allí.

Y los cabritos allá recontentos, cenando ya con la alegría, pues, de que no se los había comido el lobo. No habían muerto. Ya estaban ellos cenando cuando el lobo se agachó a tomar agua y al agacharse, como le pesaban mucho las piedras, se fue de cabeza al estanque. Y luego dicen los cabritos: —¡Aa! ¿Oyen aquel ruídazo? ¿Qué sería? Vamos a ver.

Ya fueron y se asomaron y su sorpresa fue que el lobo estaba allí hogado ya en el estanque. Ya de gusto cantaron ellos. Ya que había muerto el enemigo, que a ellos tanto les combatía y que eran libres todos los hijos. Siguieron viviendo muy felices los cabritos allí en su casa, muy contentos con su mamá.

A Granny Who Had Many Children

This story was collected in Canada from Jews who immigrated from Poland and Russia. Many of them spoke a variant of German called Yiddish. When the grandmother calls the bear "Berele" (Bear-uh-luh) she is saying a Yiddish version of the word "bear." The groats the children eat are a kind of milk and oatmeal, and when the bear gets his rear end shod it means he has the blacksmith put a big horseshoe on his seat!

*O*nce upon a time there was a Granny who had many, many children. One day Granny had to go into the woods to gather some kindling wood. She told the children that if anyone should come, they should not let him in, and warned them especially about the big bear who prowled about in the forest and sometimes came near the house.

When Granny left, the children latched all the windows, barred the door, and hid. One hid on top of the cupboard, one under the cupboard; one on the bed, one under the bed; one on top of the oven, one under the oven; one over the chimney, one under the chimney. But the tiny little Heshela just couldn't find a place to hide, so he slid into a little bottle and sat there, very still.

Just then the great big bear passed by the house and noticed that Granny had gone to the woods to gather some kindling wood. He thought: "I'll just go in and gobble up all those little children." So he knocked on the door and said: "Children, children, open the door."

No one answered.

So he said again: "Children, children, open the door and I'll give you some blackberries."

The children replied: "No. We have our own blackberries."

So the bear said: "Children, children, open the door and I'll give you some blueberries."

And the children said: "No. We have some blueberries too."

So the bear went off to the blacksmith's and had his rear end well shod, and returned. This time he said: "Children, children, if you don't open the door, I'll break it in!"

And the children answered: "We're not afraid of you! We'd rather listen to Granny!"

So the angry bear turned around and with his well-shod rear end broke the door down. He went into the house, searched out all the children, opened his great big mouth, and "hm, hm," he ate them all up!

But the tiny little Heshela, who was hiding inside the little bottle, saw everything. But the bear did not see him at all! Then the great big bear went back into the forest.

When Granny returned, she found the house very still. She called: "Children, dear children, where are you?"

No one answered. She called again: "Children, dear children, where *are* you?"

But no one answered. So she began to look everywhere for them. She looked in the corridor. No one was there. She looked in the attic. Nobody was there. So she called again and again: "Dear little children, where are you?"

Just then little Heshela crawled out of the little bottle and jumped into Granny's lap and told her the whole story: how the great big bear came out of the forest; how he broke the door down with his well-shod rear end; how he found all the children and ate them all up!

When Granny heard this, she took a great big knife. She went to the blacksmith's and had him sharpen it very well, and hid it under her apron. Then she went off into the forest and called: "Berele, Berele, come to me."

"I won't," grunted the bear.

Granny said again: "Berele, Berele, come and I will give you some delicious milk pudding."

"I won't come," growled the bear.

So Granny said, "Berele, Berele, if you come, I will tickle your ear!"

"Aha!" said the bear, "That's exactly what I like!"

And the great big bear came out of the forest and lay down on the ground and put his head in Granny's lap. Granny began to tickle his ears—first the right one and then the left one.

"Hmmmmm," said the bear, his eyes closed and his great big mouth smiling. "Hmmmmm," and he seemed to be dozing off with pleasure.

When Granny noticed this, she took the sharp knife from under her apron, and quick as anything she snipped open the bear's belly, and all the little children came tumbling out!

Granny took all the children home and washed them and scrubbed them; she combed their hair and put clean clothes on them: she let them wear their new shoes and pretty socks to match. Then she set them all on a great big shovel and said: "Whoops now, off with you—to school you go!"

Socks to wear, socks to mend,
Our little story is at an end.
Groats with milk to make you shine,
Don't you think this story's fine?

Tagaro's Fish

*I*nstead of telling about parents and children, this story tells about trying to protect one's pets. It comes from a group of islands northeast of Australia once called Melanesia. Today they're called Vanuatu. The people of these islands have many tales about Tagaro and his enemy, Mera-mbuto. It is said that Tagaro descended from heaven, created things on earth, and then returned to heaven.

*P*eople say Tagaro paddled his canoe out near a large rock in the sea. He let his canoe float free and soon many fish swam near. Instead of catching them Tagaro fed them his food and they gladly ate it.

He told the fish, "I'll be back in two days with delicious food for you and coconut sauce."

Just as he'd promised, Tagaro came back in two days and sang to them. "My nice little fish wherever you are. I've brought you special food."

Tagaro didn't know that someone was listening as he sang his song. Early the next morning Mera-mbuto, the one who had heard Tagaro sing, paddled out to the place Tagaro fed his fish. Mera-mbuto sang the song Tagaro sang, but the fish knew the voice they were hearing was too loud for Tagaro's. All the fish stayed deep in the water. When they wouldn't swim close Mera-mbuto altered his voice. When he sang the song again the fish swam to the surface and Mera-mbuto caught them all with a hook.

As fast as he could, Mera-mbuto paddled back to shore, ran to his village, built a fire, and put the fish in the oven.

When Tagaro paddled out to see his fish at the usual time he discovered all his fish were gone. He suspected the evil Mera-mbuto had caught them for food. Tagaro followed the footprints he found on shore and they took him to Mera-mbuto's.

When Tagaro arrived he acted pleasant as he could be. He walked in and asked, "What is cooking in your oven? Could you share? I'm feeling very hungry."

Mera-mbuto said his food was bad, that Tagaro shouldn't eat it.

Suddenly Tagaro jumped up and yelled, "And neither should you! Those are *my* fish and you stole them all."

Tagaro was so angry he hit Mera-mbuto and killed him. Then burned his house to the ground. Tagaro gathered all his fish from the oven and put them back in a little pool of sea water. Thanks to that, they survived. One side of each fish was gone from the cooking, but the other side was still fine. People still call them Tagaro's half-fish. Others call them soles.

The Cunning Snake

*J*oel Chandler Harris collected this tale and many others in the early 1880s from African-Americans who had lived as slaves in the United States before the Civil War. In this version two different mothers—a snake and a woman—lose their children. But instead of a wolf, fox, or bear being the greedy villain, each mother in this tale steals the other one's child.

*O*ne time an African woman was walking through the woods and fields when she found a snake's nest with a great big egg. The woman really wanted the egg, but she was afraid to take it. That night she dreamed of the egg and when she woke up she decided she had to have that egg. She went back to the nest, took the egg, and cooked it up for breakfast.

When the snake came back to her nest and found the egg gone she followed her nose and tracked the woman's trail all the way to her house. Snake slid into her house and asked for her egg. The woman said she hadn't seen any egg, but Snake saw its shell in the corner.

"What about that shell?" asked Snake.

The woman didn't say a word.

"How come you tore up my nest and took my egg?"

The woman still didn't say a word. She just shook her hair and went back to work as if the snake wasn't even there.

Snake yelled. "Woman! You took my egg and killed my child. You'd better be sure to take care of yours." Then Snake shot out her tongue and slid away.

Bye 'n bye the woman had a baby, a pretty little girl called Noncy. She hugged her with love all day, all the time. She kept her close on her back for safety's sake 'cause she remembered what angry Snake had said.

All this time Snake's been hiding in the grass. Watching all day and watching all night. Shooting out her tongue and sliding through the grass, thinking about eating that baby girl.

Bye 'n bye the baby got as big and heavy as a bag of rice, and the woman got tired of carrying her around. She got so tired she got to huffing and gasping like a caught cat-fish. The woman put the girl inside the house and showed her how to lock the door.

"Don't open the door," the woman said "till you hear me sing my song."

All the while Snake was hiding in the grass. All coiled up and waiting her time.

Bye 'n bye as night came near the woman came back and sang her song:

> *Walla walla witto, me Noncy,*
> *Walla walla witto, me Noncy,*
> *Walla walla witto, me Noncy!*

The little girl recognized the song and her mother's voice, and gladly answered back: Andolee! Andoli! Andolo!

The Cunning Snake

She pulled out the peg, opened the door and hugged her mother tight.

The next day things went the same way. And the day after that and the day after that. For seven days things went the same way. And all the while Snake hid in the bush, watching and listening as she tried to learn that song.

Bye 'n bye when the woman was gone Snake went to the door just before the woman was due to come home, and sang the song:

> *Wullo wullo widdo, me Noncy,*
> *Wullo wullo widdo, me Noncy,*
> *Wullo wullo widdo, me Noncy!*

She tried to sing it sweet like the woman did, but her voice was rough and big. The girl said, "No. Go away. *My* mother doesn't sing like that."

Snake tried three more times, but the girl said no. Snake finally slid away, but she still meant to learn that song.

When the woman came back Snake listened hard as she sang:

> *Walla walla witto, me Noncy,*
> *Walla walla witto, me Noncy,*
> *Walla walla witto, me Noncy!*

The little girl sang right back and opened the door:

> *Andolee! Andoli! Andolo!*

All day the next day Snake thought about that song. She practiced saying it forward in her mind and backwards, too. When it was nearing sundown again Snake went to the door and sang the song:

> *Walla walla witto, me Noncy,*
> *Walla walla witto, me Noncy,*
> *Walla walla witto, me Noncy!*

This time Snake sounded just like the woman. The girl sang right back and opened the door.

Andolee! Andoli! Andolo!

She ran to hug her mother, but Snake twisted up and caught her in a coil. She squealed and hollered, but nobody came. Snake squeezed her tight, then swallowed her whole without breaking a bone.

Bye 'n bye the woman came home and sang her song. When nobody answered she started to tremble and shake. When she pushed the door open and saw that her girl was gone she cried and hollered, "Oh why did somebody take my girl?" Then she saw Snake's trail on the road.

"That snake!" she hollered. "That snake came and swallowed my sweet little girl."

She quickly cut a cane from the swamp and started tracking down Snake. The woman was so mad she went streaking along. Snake was so full she couldn't go fast and she soon got so sleepy she just laid down and closed her eyes.

Real soon the woman came by. When she saw Snake asleep on the ground she fast, broke her head with her cane and mashed her flat. Then fast as she could she cut Snake open and found her girl who looked just like she'd been taking a nap. The woman took her home, washed her off and as soon as the little girl opened her eyes the mother sang her song and Noncy sang back:

Andolee! Andoli! Andolo!

The Goat, the Kids, and the Wolf

*T*his tale was recorded from a 79-year-old peasant woman in France over thirty years ago. Other French versions were published as long ago as 1886. In some of these tales the animals are chickens and pigs instead of goats. In this story the wolf is so greedy he tries to eat the goats' cheese-cake, too. The goat's cheese-cake is more like a cake stuffed with cheese than the dessert many eat in the United States.

There was a nanny goat who had broken her leg. She had to go and have it set at Saint Jard. She had to leave her little kids behind, and she said to them, "I am going off to have my leg set at Saint Jard. Don't open the door to anyone. When I come back I shall say to you:

> Little kid and she kid,
> Open the door for you mother,
> Who comes from St. Jard,
> Where she's had her leg and ankle set.
> Up you get, as if straw tickled your bottoms!

And then I shall show you my white leg. You'll know it's your mother, and you will open the door."

The kids knew quite well that they mustn't open that door. However, the wolf heard what the nanny goat said to her kids. He came to their door and said to them:

> Little kid and little she kid,
> Open the door for you mother,
> Who comes from St. Jard,
> Where she's had her leg and ankle set.
> Up you get, as if straw tickled your bottoms!

But the nanny goat had said to her kids that a white leg must be shown.

The little kids shouted through the door, "Show your white leg!"

The wolf put his leg through a hole, perhaps it was through the cat hole. (You know, of course, that there were cat holes in the doors in the old days.)

The kids saw that he had a black leg. "Oh," they said, "you have a black leg! You are not our mother."

The wolf went and dipped his leg in flour, which was nice and white, and he came back and knocked on the little kids' door, saying once again:

> Little kid and little she kid,
> Open the door for your mother,
> Who comes from St. Jard,
> Where she's had her leg and ankle set.
> Up you get, as if straw tickled your bottoms!

The kids said, "Show your leg!"

So then he had a beautiful white leg. The little kids opened the door, and the wolf was in their home.

"If you have something to eat, give it to me at once, or else I shall eat you."

The kids were so frightened that they did not know what to do. The wolf asked them if they had any *froumajhé* (cheesecake) in the dough bin to give him to eat.

Now it so happened that the nanny goat had just made cheesecake, which she had put into the dough bin next to the cheeses so that the cakes would keep cool. Well, now, you won't believe this. The wolf leaped into the dough bin, the greedy thing, intent on eating the cheesecake. So then the little kids had closed the lid of the dough bin, and the wolf was so busy eating that he took no notice.

When the nanny goat arrived, she knocked at the door, saying:

> *Little kid and little she kid,*
> *Open the door for you mother,*
> *Who comes from St. Jard,*
> *Where she's had her leg and ankle set.*
> *Up you get, as if straw tickled your bottoms!*

The kids ran to open the door for her.

"Do you know, the wolf came. He showed us a white leg, so we opened the door, and then he wanted to eat cheesecake. He went into the dough bin, so we closed the lid on top of him."

The nanny goat said they had done the right thing. "Wait a minute! We must put some water on to boil in the stewpot."

The wolf began yelling, "Open the lid of the dough bin!"

"Make some holes in the dough bin," said the nanny goat to her kids.

The little kids pierced the lid, and the wolf was able to breathe more easily. As soon as the holes were finished, the water began to boil over the fire. Then the nanny goat took the handle of the kettle and poured water through the holes in the lid.

The wolf tried to get out of the way, first one side then the other, but he could not escape. Try as he might, in the end he was scalded by the nanny goat.

When they had poured out the whole kettle, the nanny goat lifted the lid of the dough bin and the wolf hurled himself out.

Then the nanny goat stood on the threshhold and shouted:

> *The running wolf is on his way!*
> *Watch out, shepherdesses in the hay!*
> *The scalded wolf is on the run!*
> *Watch out, shepherdesses every one!*

When a Wise Man Dies, a Wise Man Buries Him

*L*ike other variants, this tale is written in a different kind of English than is spoken in the United States. It comes from Cameroon, a country on the west coast of Africa, and is different in three major ways. Instead of a mother protecting her child, a child protects his mother. Tortoise hides his mother high in the clouds rather than inside a house, and the villain must call for the rope to climb rather than knock at the door.

This is the story of a time when there was a famine in the whole country. It's very funny, so listen carefully.

There was a famine in the country. The famine was terrible. So all the animals in the forest decided that they must do something and they must do it immediately. So now, they called a meeting. They said: "What will we do now? There is no food in the country. What will we do?"

Then one animal said: "There's only one thing that we can do. Before we die, let us eat our mothers. They have already had their life. Let us eat them one by one before we die."

So they discussed it a great deal and they agreed saying: "Yes, you've got intelligence. We shall all die if we don't eat our mothers. It will be hard to eat them, but they have already given us life once, they will agree to give it to us again. The thing will be really hard but we shall eat our mothers."

So now, Tortoise was at this meeting. He listened to the things they said. He thought and thought about it and he was very sad because he loved his mother very much, and he didn't want them to eat her. He thought and thought and said: "Unh, unh! What kind of a thing is this! Eat our mothers! I could eat their mothers but I couldn't eat my own mother." Then he thought: "That's what I'll do!" So he took his mother and hid her in the clouds. He said he couldn't eat her. So Tortoise gave his mother a basket. He tied it onto a long rope. He told her he would come every single day and bring her a little meat. He would come with in and call his mother saying: "Mammy, send down the chain, Mammy, send down the chain."

So when his mother would hear that she could send down the chain, letting it down, then Tortoise would put a little food inside, food that he had kept for her, then he would tell his mother: "Pull up the chain, Mammy, pull up the chain."

The next day they came and took Leopard's mother to the (meeting) place. They ate her. Every man ate to his heart's content. They didn't notice that Tortoise took a little to keep aside. Then Tortoise went off, stood under that cloud and said: "Send down the chain, Mammy, send down the chain." Mammy Tortoise sent down the chain, Tortoise put the food inside and said: "Pull up the chain, Mammy, pull up the chain." So Tortoise's mother was there. She was fine. Nobody knew that Tortoise took a little beef to give her some.

So now, they took their mothers and ate them. Every single day they were eating somebody's mother. One day they ate Lion's mother. One day they ate Elephant's mother and they thought they would never eat again. Then they ate Monkey's mother and she was terribly thin. So now, every single day they ate until they had almost finished their mothers entirely.

Tortoise knew that soon they would come and say: "Bring your own mother." So one day now, he came to that place. He cried with loud shouts, he cried and said: "Wey! This is terrible today o! Mammy has died. Mammy has died. She didn't eat for so long that hunger killed her. Why don't you come and see the small grave that I put her in."

The animals went and looked at the spot. Tortoise had put a stone in the grave. They said: "Ashia! We share in your sorrow."

Then they said: "Ashia, o! But don't cry too much. Don't you know that if she hadn't died we would have had to eat her. Come, let's eat."

So they went off, but Hare didn't like it at all. He thought that perhaps it was a ruse. So he didn't say anything but he watched how Tortoise ate a little and kept aside a little, ate a little kept aside a little. So he thought: "So that's what he's doing. What will he do with the food he isn't eating?"

So Hare followed behind Tortoise. He saw Tortoise go to the cloud and say: "Send down the chain, Mammy, send down the chain." Mammy Tortoise sent down the chain. Tortoise put the food in the basket. Then he said: "Pull up the chain, Mammy, pull up the chain."

Hare ran and told the other animals. They agreed: "That's not nice. Tortoise won't fool us. He is not going to come and eat our mothers and keep his own on a cloud." They went on: "We must do something." They decided that they would wait until Tortoise was asleep. Because when he had gone and given his mother the food, the action contented his heart, then he was able to sleep well. So they decided to watch Tortoise. Then when he was asleep they would go and speak to Mammy Tortoise saying: "Send down the chain, Mammy, send down the chain." Then, when she had sent it down they would get inside the basket and call out: "Pull up the chain, Mammy, pull up the chain." Then, Mammy would pull them all up. They would all go up. They would meet his mother and they would eat her.

So they went to the cloud where Mammy Tortoise was. Leopard said: "Send down the chain, Mammy, send down the chain."

Mammy Tortoise listened carefully: "Uhn, uhn. That's not Tortoise's voice o!" Mammy Tortoise was intelligent too. So she didn't agree to send down the chain. So Hare said: "Your voice is too big. You must go to the blacksmith so that he can reduce your voice, so that he can knock it until it is very small."

When a Wise Man Dies, a Wise Man Buries Him

So now, Leopard went to the blacksmith. The blacksmith hit his voice, hit it, hit it, hit the thing. But the voice was not very small. No indeed! Anyway, they went back. They said they would try again. So Leopard called out: "Send down the chain, Mammy, send down the chain." Mammy thought: "Uhn, uhn. It's not Tortoise's voice, That's not my child's voice." And Mammy began to wonder what was happening.

So now, they said: "You must go again to that blacksmith. Let him reduce your voice a little. The thing ach! The thing is too big." So he went again to the blacksmith, and asked him to knock his voice. He knocked it, knocked it, knocked it, knocked, four good bangs he gave it. The animals listened to the voice. And they said it would do. So now, Leopard had suffered a great deal in connection with this voice but they thought that it would do. So they went to Mammy Tortoise's cloud. Leopard spoke very quietly saying: "Send down the chain, Mammy, send down the chain." Mammy listened: "Send down the chain, Mammy, send down the chain." The voice was now small and Mammy Tortoise thought it was Tortoise.

So now, the mother sent down the chain. All the animals were glad. They decided that they would jump into the basket. Then the mother would pull them up. They would all go up. So they jumped into the basket to let Mammy begin to pull them up. So when Mammy began to pull them up now, the basket was very heavy. She pulled it up a little, then she rested. The basket was so heavy! She wondered: "What kind of plentiful food is this child sending me?"

So now, the mother pulled. The basket was heavy. All the animals were in the basket. They were hanging thus. And Tortoise was sleeping but something just told him that everything was not all right. Tortoise got up. He ran to see Leopard in his house. Leopard was not there. He ran to see Hare. Hare was not there. He ran to see to his mother. He saw how that poor Mammy was struggling to pull up the basket. He shouted. He told his mother: "It's not me, Mammy, it's not me." He called out: "It wasn't me who called you, Mammy, it wasn't me." Then he shouted: "Don't pull, Mammy. Cut the chain, Mammy, cut the chain." He shouted it again and again: "Cut the chain, Mammy. Cut the chain."

So now Mammy tried her best. She looked at the chain. She found one link that was not too thick. She found a big stone and banged it against the chain cutting it at one go.

So all those animals fell to the ground. They died immediately. Tortoise and his mother ate all that meat and the famine didn't ever hurt them again.

I tell you all those Tortoises have a great deal of intelligence.

La Belle Venus

"*L*a Belle Venus" comes from Haiti, an island country in the Caribbean Sea. This version has no animal characters or typical villains. Instead it reflects the extreme differences between Haiti's poor and wealthy people. When a wealthy young man sends his servants to find a star they discover a poor girl. Romance, rather than hunger, brings the deceitful knock at the door, and the man is so rich he has someone else do his knocking.

*T*here was once a young woman named Mimi who was very comely and who worked for the family of Roy, where she had a good position and met many people. One day she met a handsome man called Gro Neg, whom she talked with many times. Gro Neg eventually asked her to marry him but wanted her to keep her place with the family of Roy.

So Mimi and Gro Neg were married and lived very happily for a while, until one day Gro Neg went away and was never heard from again. At first Mimi became very sad, but she was consoled when she learned she was to have a child.

Away into the country she went and built a house and it was there that she had her baby—a girl—alone. No one knew about her house nor about her child. The little girl was so beautiful that Mimi called her La Belle Venus. She was born with a star on her forehead which shone with a brilliant light.

Mimi and La Belle Venus lived very contentedly while the little girl was small, but when she began to grow up Mimi feared for her daughter, because she was so beautiful, and because Mimi had to leave her alone all day while she went to work at the house of Roy.

Then between them they devised a song which Mimi sang each time she came to the house, so that La Belle Venus would open the door only for her. The song went like this:

> *La Belle Venus, La Belle Venus, leve deshabilles,*
> *La Belle Venus, ouvert la porte lá.*

And La Belle Venus would answer:

> *Ye, ye, la porte s'ouvre.*

Even after Mimi had taught the child all this she was still afraid and continually cautioned her.

"Be very careful each time that it is I singing. Other people may try to enter here." And with this warning she would leave for work.

Now the wife of Monsieur Roy, who was a very grand lady, one day had some special sewing to be done. It was very delicate work and she did not know anyone who could do it. Mimi had taught La Belle Venus to use a needle exceedingly well and so she offered to have the sewing done for Madame Roy.

"Good," Madame Roy said. "If it is done well I will give you half of all the money I own, but if it is done poorly I am afraid you will have to pay with your life."

"Never fear—it will be done well," Mimi promised, and she took the sewing away with her.

La Belle Venus spent many days, while her mother was away at work, sewing on the fine cloth for Madame Roy. When it was finished Mimi looked it over very carefully and saw that it was done even better than she had expected. Then she brought it to Madame Roy.

"It is well done, indeed," Madame Roy told Mimi; "here is the money I promised you."

Mimi thanked her and that evening when she arrived home buried the money in her garden, because she wanted some day to buy a piano for La Belle Venus.

Now the Roys had a son, whose name was Rénault. He was very proud and very handsome and his mother and father had given him all the things he wished for. One night before he went to bed he saw a very big and very beautiful star shining in the woods. It was not like the other stars, and Rénault went to his father and said to him, "Father, there is a star in the woods which is so beautiful that I long to have it for my own."

Roy loved his son above all else and wanted to please him, but he did not know how he could manage to get a star for him. Nevertheless, that night he sent a man into the woods to search for the bright star which Rénault had seen. Later the man returned with a strange story.

"In the woods," he told Monsieur Roy, "I came upon a little house set among the trees, but when I went to the door no one came to answer my knock. I walked behind the house and in the garden I saw a girl. When I called to her she turned to me and I was blinded by the shining star on her forehead."

"This is indeed strange," Roy said. "I must see this for myself. Bring the girl here."

"I tried to talk to her," the man told him, "but she ran away while I was still blinded and I do not know where she can be found."

"You must bring her here," Monsieur Roy said, "or I shall have you punished."

"I will look again," the man promised, and he went to the woods near the house where he had seen La Belle Venus and hid himself among the trees and bushes.

He hid there a long time before Mimi came home and sang:

> *La Belle Venus, La Belle Venus, leve deshabilles,*
> *La Belle Venus, ouvert la porte lá.*

Then La Belle Venus answered her:

Ye, ye, la porte s'ouvre.

And he saw the door open and Mimi go inside. Now he knew how he could get into the house, but he had to wait for Mimi to leave so he could sing the song and be admitted. He waited all that night, then on the next afternoon while Mimi was away he went to the door and sang the song. But his voice was coarse and La Belle Venus did not recognize it and would not open the door.

The man was very put out and went to Roy and told him he would have to have money to get medicine to change his voice. He told his master about the house and the song he had to sing to get in, and Roy gave him the money for the medicine.

After going to the medicine man he took the pill which was given to him to make his voice soft and high like a woman's and swallowed it. He then went into the woods again and hid in the bushes, waiting for La Belle Venus to be alone. While he waited he became very hungry and looked about for something to eat. He found some fruit and ate it.

Finally he saw Mimi go away and he went to the door and tried to sing the song that would make La Belle Venus open the door. He sang, but his voice was a coarse as ever and he then remembered that he should not have eaten anything after taking the pill— he had been told that if he did, it would not work—so there was nothing for him to do but go back and ask for more money to get another pill from the medicine man. Roy was very angry and said to him:

"If you do not bring the beautiful girl tomorrow I will put you in prison."

This time the man remembered to eat something *before* he took the pill. Then he went to the woods and waited for the girl to be alone again. When he was sure that Mimi had gone he sang the song. His voice was high and sweet, so without even looking the girl answered and opened the door.

When the door opened the man was standing close by and he seized La Belle Venus before the shining star could blind him. He carried her in his arms through the woods and toward the house of Roy. La Belle Venus was very much afraid because she had never seen anyone but her mother before. She was crying and shaking with fright when the man took her into the house of Roy.

Monsieur Roy and everyone in the house immediately became blinded by the beauty of La Belle Venus and the shining star on her brow.

"You shall have your reward," Roy told the man, "but the girl is too beautiful; I do not know how anyone can possibly live near her."

He then called his son, Rénault, to tell him that he had found the bright, strange star for him. When Rénault came into the room he looked at La Belle Venus, but he was not blinded by the star. He saw the most beautiful girl he had ever seen and fell to his knees in front of her.

"Father," he said, "she is most wonderful and I want her for my wife."

"So it shall be," his father said, because he wanted his son to be happy.

Mimi, when she learned of what had passed, was very pleased with the good fortune of La Belle Venus and helped with the preparations for the wedding. Roy built a fine house for the young couple and gave it to them as a dowry. It was built high on a mountain—so that La Belle Venus' beauty would not blind the people of the town. Rénault bought a piano for her.

They still live in the house and are very, very happy. You can look up any evening into the mountain where they live and see the bright star of La Belle Venus shining forth as she walks with Rénault in the garden.

La Belle Venus

Tiger Softens His Voice

*L*ike "The Devil Hammers His Tongue" and "When a Wise Man Dies . . ." this tale is written in a dialect or different kind of English than that spoken in the United States. The story itself has traveled a great deal. Martha Warren Beckwith collected it from a man living in Jamaica, an island south of Cuba and Florida. He heard it while visiting Cape Coast, Ghana, in Africa. Tiger is the villain, and, like the wealthy man in "La Belle Venus," he has marriage in mind.

*O*nce upon a time a woman had one daughter, an' that daughter was the prettiest girl in an' around that country. Every man want the girl to marry, but the mother refuse them as they come. Tiger, too, wanted the girl, an' demands the girl, an' the mother says no. Tiger said if he don't get the girl he will kill her. So they remove from that part of the country and go to another part, into a thick wild wood where no one live. And she made a house with a hundred doors and a hundred windows and a large staircase; and the house is an upstairs, an' there both of them live.

Tiger hear of it, always loafing aroun' the house to see if he can catch the girl, but the girl never come out. During the day, the mother went to her work, leaving the girl at home. When going out, the mother fasten all the doors an' windows; coming home in the evening, at a certain spot where she can see the house an' notice that all the windows an' doors are close as she leave it, then now she have a song to sing, go like this,—

Tom Jones, Tom Jones, Tom Jones!

(that's the name of the girl). Girl now—

Deh lo, madame!

Woman said to her now,

Fare you well, fare you well, fare you well,
Fare you well, me dear; fare you well, me love!
A no Tiger, deh la, ho, deh la, ho?
Me jus' come, ho!

Then the door open, so—

Checky checky knock umbar,
Checky checky knock umbar,
Checky checky knock umbar.

The door don't open without that song now, and when it open, the mamma go into the house.

At that same time, Tiger in the bush listening to the song. So one day while she was away, hear time for her to come home, Tiger approach the spot where she always sing. He now in a very coarse voice sings the song,—

Tom Jones, Tom Jones, Tom Jones!

Tiger Softens His Voice

The girl look from the window, said, "Tiger, a who no know sa' a you!" So now Tiger go 'way an' hide till mamma come. When she come, he listen good. Next day, Tiger go to a blacksmith an' ask de blacksmith what he t'ink can give him, Tiger, a clear v'ice. De blacksmit' say he must hot a long iron an' when it hot, mus' take it push down his t'roat. An' de blacksmit' give him a bit of meat to eat after he burn the throat an' that will give him a clear v'ice. So Tiger go away eat de meat first an' den burn de t'roat after. Nex' day he went to the spot where the woman always sing from. An' that make his v'ice more coarser. He sing now—

Tom Jones, Tom Jones, Tom Jones!

The girl thru the window an' say, "Cho! a who no know sa' a you!" So Tiger got vex' now, an' he went home, burn the throat first and afterward eat the meat, and that give him a clearer v'ice than the woman. The nex' day, when most time for the woman to come home from her work, Tiger went to the spot where he can see the house. He begin to sing,

Tom Jones, Tom Jones, Tom Jones!

The girl answer (tho't it was her mother now)—

Deh la, madame!

Then Tiger say,

> *Fare you well, fare you well, fare you well,*
> *Fare you well, me dear; fare you well, me love!*
> *A no Tiger deh lo o-o-o*
> *Me jus come, h-o-o-o!*

The door commence to open now,—

> *Checky checky checky knock umbar,*
> *Checky checky checky knock umbar,*
> *Checky checky checky knock umbar!*

And as the door open, Tiger step up an' caught the girl an' swallow her.

And when the mother coming home, reach to the spot and saw the doors and windows open, she throw down what she carry and run to the house. And she saw Tiger lay down. And the mother then went away an' get some strong men come an' tie Tiger, kill him, an' open de belly an' take out de daughter. At that time, little life left in her an' they get back the life in her. The woman then leave the house an' go off away far into another country, and that is why you always fin' lot of old houses unoccupied that no one live in.

The Jackal and the Lambs

*T*his tale was collected from the Kabyl people in Algeria, a country in North Africa and on the Mediterranean Sea. Sheep are the main characters, and they live in a small cave called a grotto instead of a house. Jackal—a type of wild dog—is the sheep's natural enemy and the villain who knocks at the door. As in other versions, insects play a vital role, but here they help the villain rather than the mother and children.

*A*ewe had two lambs in a grotto which served her as a house. Every day the ewe went to pasture, grazed, then tore up grass and carried it home between her horns. When she reached the grotto she knocked on the door and called: "The jug between the legs (udder) and the hay between the horns!" This sentence was the password. When the young lambs heard it they knew their mother was outside. So then they opened the door and their mother came in carrying the hay between her horns. The ewe often said to the young lambs: "You must never open the door to anyone but me. You can recognize me by what I say and by my voice." The young lambs promised.

One day the ewe came home as usual with the bundle of hay on her horns, knocked on the door of the grotto and called: "The jug between the legs and the hay between the horns." The little lambs opened the door. Nearby in the bush was the jackal. He heard what the ewe said and he saw the lambs and he said to himself: "That would make a nice meal for me. I'll visit those lambs tomorrow."

The next day the jackal went to the grotto, knocked on the door and called: "The jug between the legs and the hay between the horns." The two lambs heard his words and they noticed his voice. They said to each other: "That is not our mother. We had better not open the door." They ran to the door and called to the jackal: "We do not know your voice and we are not going to open the door." The jackal ran off.

The jackal went to a wise man and said: "What can I do to have a voice as soft as a ewe's?" The wise man said: "Go lie on an ant heap. Let the ants run in and out of your mouth. The ants will eat away part of your throat so that it will become quite small, like that of a sheep." The jackal thanked him and left.

The jackal ran to an ant heap. He laid himself on the ant heap. The ants ran in and out of his mouth and ate away part of his throat. His throat grew small like that of a sheep. His voice grew soft. Towards evening the jackal went again to the grotto where the young lambs were, knocked on the door and called: "The jug between the legs and the hay between the horns." The young lambs heard him. They said to each other: "That is our mother's voice." They ran to the door. They opened the door. The jackal entered. He devoured the two young lambs and then ran off to the forest. When the ewe came home she found the door open. She found no lambs. She said: "That must have been the jackal."

The ewe went as usual to the pasture to graze. She tore up grass and loaded a bundle on her horns. In the evening she brought home her bundle of hay between her horns. One day she saw the jackal. Quickly she threw her bundle of hay at the jackal. The jackal lay buried beneath the hay. The ewe laid herself on the hay. Then she called the shepherd. The shepherd came. The ewe said: "Here under this hay lies the jackal who killed my lambs." The shepherd took his crook and beat the jackal to death.

The Ewe, the Goat and the Lion

*L*ike "The Story of the Wolf and the Goat" (Iran), the mother in this tale gets help by giving a thoughtful gift. The tale comes from the Jewish people who lived in Kurdistan, an area of rugged mountains that overlaps Turkey, Iran, and Iraq. When Lion, the villain, gives the judge a balloon, it is one made from an animal's bladder, which was used in ancient times instead of rubber, which we use in balloons today.

*T*here were once a ewe and a goat. The ewe was very fond of the goat and the goat was likewise fond of the ewe. One day the ewe said to the goat, "Let us build a house for ourselves. Rainy days will come soon, and without a shelter we will have no place to hide ourselves from the rains."

The goat would not listen to the ewe and rejected her suggestion. The ewe then appealed to another goat, but was again rebuffed. What could the ewe do? She began to build the house relying on herself alone. However, during the construction she appealed again to the goat, "Let us build a common house for ourselves." But her suggestion was once more rejected.

The ewe continued her work alone until it was successfully finished. A few days later the rainy season began. One day, as torrential rain was pouring down, the goat came by and pleaded with the ewe, "Please let me sleep one night with you in the shelter." But the ewe rejected his plea, and the goat had to spend the night outdoors. The next day the ewe came out of her house, and behold, the goat was lying outside dead and lifeless.

The ewe decided to use the goat's carcass to build a new and stronger house. His hide served as a tent cloth, his legs as columns, and so forth. All in all, the house was very beautiful.

When spring arrived the ewe gave birth to two lambs and named them Anjula and Banjula. Whenever the ewe went outside to graze she would lock the lambs indoors, and only in the evening, when she returned home, would she call out, "Anjula, Banjula, open the door! Your mother is back and has a lot of milk for you." The lambs would then open the door, and the ewe would feed them her milk.

This continued for a month or two, until one day the lion noticed it and decided to kill and eat the lambs. But how was he to do it? How should he carry out his evil plan? Finally he found a solution: he decided to disguise himself as the ewe, approach the house, and ask the lambs to open the door for him. The lambs would think that this time their mother had returned early and would open the door.

So the lion went to the ewe's house and called out, "Anjula, Banjula, open the door! Your mother is back and has a lot of milk for you." The lambs replied, "Our mother does not return so early," and the lion retorted, "Today there was a lot of herbage, and I managed to eat quickly." The lambs replied, "Our mother has long ears, small legs, and is white, whereas you are very strange looking."

So the lion went away, dyed himself with a white dye, and returned to the lambs, but this time too the lambs refused to open the door. What did the lion do? He broke the door open and killed and ate both lambs.

In the evening the mother returned home and called, "Anjula, Banjula, open the door! Your mother is back and has a lot of milk for you." No answer and no response. The ewe repeated her call two and three times, but there was still no response. She then pushed the door open, and what did she see? The house was empty. The ewe did not know what to do.

She went to the fox's house and cried out, "Fox, fox, come out and fight me! Why did you take my sons?" The fox came out, saying, "I did not take your sons, ewe—I have no reason to fight you."

The ewe then went to the chicken coop, and the chickens woke up and began clucking out of fear of the ewe. The ewe called out to them, "You have taken my lambs. Come out and fight me!" The chickens replied, "We did not take your lambs—we have no reason to fight you."

The ewe then came down the chicken coop's roof to the dog's lair, and the dog came out, asking, "What do you want from me, ewe?" The ewe said, "You have taken my two lambs from me. Come out now and fight me!" The dog replied, "I have not taken your lambs, ewe—I am not going to fight you."

Finally, the ewe went to the lion's den, and he came out and roared, "Who is it that wakes me up from my slumber? Who is disturbing my sleep?" The ewe replied, "It is I who am disturbing you, and I shall continue to do so. Why did you kill my lambs? Come out now and fight me!" The lion replied, "I have indeed killed your children, but I will not fight you until we go to the judge and hear his decision."

The ewe consented, and both of them agreed on a date for the trial. The ewe prepared a bowl of white, fresh, and wholesome milk as a gift for the judge. The lion, too, took a large balloon, painted it nicely, put in it four seeds of wheat, inflated it, and took it to the judge's house to give to him as a gift.

The lion and the ewe entered the judge's house and greeted him, and the judge returned their greetings. All three sat down. The ewe handed the judge the milk bowl, saying, "This is all I can give you," while the lion gave the balloon to the judge's wife, saying, "This is all I could bring you."

The curious woman could not restrain her desire to know what was inside the balloon, and as she began opening it, a seed was suddenly blown out and struck the judge's eyes with such force that he was blinded. The next seed struck the wife's eyes and she too was blinded. The third seed struck the wall and made a hole in it, and the fourth one struck the door and made a hole in it too.

What did the judge do? He fetched a pair of pincers and pulled out all the lion's teeth. He then sharpened the ewe's horns until they were as sharp as lances. Then he turned to both contestants and announced to them, "My sentence is that you must contend in battle with each other."

So first the lion bit the ewe, but his bite was weak, for he no longer had his teeth. When it was the ewe's turn, she gored the lion in his stomach, for her horns were now very sharp. And behold, out of the lion's belly came forth the two lambs, Anjula and Banjula, alive and well.

The Water of Ladi

"*T*he Water of Ladi" from the Hausa people of Nigeria in Africa is different in several ways from other tales with a knock at the door. First, a brother is protecting his sister instead of a mother hiding her children. Second, he gets the help of many animals by using a magic calabash (a kind of dried gourd) to kidnap their drinking water. The hyena who devours the sister is one of only a few female villains in tales with a knock at the door.

T his story is about the water of Ladi. A certain hunter made a hut in the middle of the bush. He begat two children. He died and left them, a girl and a boy. And so they lived; and always the man (when) he went to hunt (and) left his sister in the house, took thorns, (and) shut up the entrance to the door. If he returned from the bush then he said, "Fatsimata, Fatsimata, Magira, open the door for me to enter, Magira. Open the door for me to enter, to come out, the elephant of the town." Always if he came from the bush he used to do this. Now of a truth the hyena overheard (him). One day he went to the bush. Then the hyena came and said, "Fajimata, Fajimata, Majia, open je door for me to enter, the elephant of je town." But the girl said, "No, I have known you, you are the hyena." Then the hyena went off, (and) went to the lion. She received from the lion medicine for curing a lisp, and came back, (and) said, "Fatsimata, Fatsimata, Magira, open the door that I may enter, Magira, open the door that I may enter, that I may come out, the elephant of the town." So the maiden opened the door, and the hyena seized her, (and) swallowed her. And the elder brother of the girl returned from the bush and said, "Fatsimata, Fatsimata, Magira, open the door for me, Magira, open the door for me to enter, to come out, the elephant of the town." Then he was silent; he repeated it again; he did not hear her answer, till (he repeated the words) three times, then he tried hard (and) opened the door. He entered, he did not see the maiden. Then he came out, lifted his calabash, and travelled until he reached the mouth of the hyena's den. He saw the girl's waist-beads and cloth lying at the mouth of the hole. And he said, "This thing the hyena did," and he passed on. Now there was a certain pool where all the wild animals of the place were wont to drink water. And he went there, there was no other water but this. He lifted up his magic calabash and scooped up all the water there, (and) went and climbed up a tree and was sitting there. Then a herd of elephants came, (and) were going to drink the water, when he said (to one), "You there, elephant, where are you going to?" She replied, "I am going to the water of Ladi." And he said, "The water of Ladi has dried up. When you have given up to me the one who ate my sister, then I have given you back the water of Ladi." So the elephant brought up the grass she had eaten, saying, "Hab! you have seen what I ate, what is inside me now is only my stomach." And the elephant passed on and went, (and) lay down, she was panting. A herd of bush-cows came up, and the boy said (to one), "You, bush-cow, where are you going?" And she said, "I am going to the water of Ladi." He said, "The water of Ladi has dried. When you have given me him who has eaten my sister, then I have given you the water of Ladi." Then the bush-cow said, "Hab! you have seen what I ate, what is inside is only my stomach." Whatever herd of wild animals came it was so; he used to ask them, (and) they too made answer so, and then passed on, (and) went to the edge of the pool, and lay down (and) were panting, until all the wild animals in the bush had passed. There remained the house of the hyena. Then they came up; the hyena which had eaten his sister was in front; she was in great haste to come (and) drink water. And he said, "You, hyena, where are you going?" And she said, "I am going to the water of Ladi." He said, "The water of Ladi is dried up. If you have given me the one who ate my sister then I have given you the water of Ladi." Silence reigned until (he had repeated it) three times. She did not answer. But the lion got angry, and he sprang, (and) caught her, (and) tore her in two, and the maiden came forth. And the lion said, "Behold your sister." So he (the hunter) poured out the water for them because he had found his sister alive. Thereupon the wild beasts began to rush the water to drink, the great ones trampled on the little ones, many died. And the boy got down from up above when they had dispersed; he collected meat, till he was weary. He went to another town and summoned help. They too collected meat till they even left some there (there was so much). That is it. Off with the rat's head.

Carlanco

*T*he villain in this story from Spain is Carlanco, a wild, scruffy, cannibalistic creature. Like the Japanese Yamauba in "The Golden Chain from Heaven," Carlanco is mean but can still be tricked by cleverness. As in many folktales, a small animal who is helped by the main character in the beginning of the story later saves the day by doing a favor in return.

*O*nce in Spain there lived a goat who was the best mother any child could have. Her house was so cleaned it seemed to shine. All three of her children were well-behaved and never went where they were told not to go.

One day as the mother goat was out gathering wood for the fire she saw a wasp that was caught in the stream and about to drown. Quick as she could, the mother goat held out a branch and brought the wasp to safety.

"Thank you," said the wasp. "Your mercy is great. If you ever need help please come to me. I live in the crumbling walls of a convent of wasps. If you need me, come ask for the Abbess. Be well. Farewell."

The wasp flew home singing her morning prayers and the kind mother goat went home to her children.

One morning the mother goat told her little kids, "Today I must go farther from the house to gather our wood. As soon as I'm gone you must lock and bar the door. Don't open it for anyone but me. The terrible ogre Carlanco might be around and hungry for sweet little kids like you. Don't open the door till you hear me sing:

> *Open the door, please open for me,*
> *For I am the mother of all you three.*

As soon as the mother goat left the house her three little kids locked the door exactly as they'd been told to do. Before long there came a knock at the door that banged so loud the whole house shook. Then a loud, ragged voice began to call,

> *The Carlanco is here so open the door,*
> *Open the door and open it now!*

The little kids hid in the corners, but called out strong, "Open it yourself if you're so strong!"

The Carlanco banged and threw himself against the door, but he couldn't get in. He finally went stomping and screaming away.

Later that day the mother goat came home and sang just as she'd told her kids she would do.

> *Open the door, please open for me,*
> *For I am the mother of all you three.*

When the kids heard her song they eagerly opened the door and let her in. It went this way several days in a row. Till one day the Carlanco hid in the bushes and heard the song and the mother goat's voice.

After the mother goat left the next morning the Carlanco sang the song to the three little kids and sang it sweetly in the mother's voice,

> *Open the door, please open for me,*
> *For I am the mother of all you three.*

Just as they had every day before when they heard those words and gentle voice the three little kids unlocked the door. And as soon as they did, the ogre Carlanco jumped into their house.

The little kids ran as fast as they could, up the ladder to the attic room. Then faster than that they pulled up the ladder behind them. The Carlanco raged even more than before and banged through the house till the little kids shook with fright. He could stretch up and see them, but couldn't quite reach them which only made him wilder.

When the mother goat came home she sang to her kids like she always did, but the door stayed shut. When she sang again they cried from the attic, "The ogre Carlanco has trapped us inside and means to eat us all."

The mother goat threw down her wood and ran faster than she'd ever run before. She ran to the convent of wasps and knocked on the door.

The innkeeper wasp said, "Go away you goat. Be off and don't come bother us here."

"Call the Abbess," ordered the mother goat. "Or I'll get the wasp-hunter I saw coming here."

Frightened by the threat the innkeeper wasp quickly got the Abbess. As soon as the Abbess heard the mother goat's words she said, "Go home and all will be well."

Before the mother goat was even halfway home the wasp had flown in through the key hole and begun to sting the Carlanco. She stung him like needles on the eyes, the nose, the ears and more, till he broke down the door and ran screaming away.

The Rabbit and the Bear

*T*his tale comes from German immigrants who settled in Pennsylvania in the early 1800s. "The Rabbit and the Bear" might well have come to the United States and been shared with children here before the Brothers Grimm published their German version, "The Wolf and the Seven Little Kids," in 1813. As in "Carlanco" and "The Story of Demane and Demazana," insects play a vital role in punishing the villain.

Once there was a rabbit who built a nest and had four little rabbits. Whenever she left the nest she warned them not to let anyone in who didn't have white paws like her.

Each time she came back she'd call to them. "I'm back with leaves and milk for you."

Her little rabbits would always say, "Show us your paw." Then she'd show her white paw and they'd let her in.

One day Bear came to their nest while their mother was away. "I'm back," he called, "with leaves and milk for you."

As they always did the rabbits said, "Show us your paw."

Bear did, but his paw was black instead of white so the rabbits refused to let him in.

Fast as he could Bear ran to the mill and had his paws all covered with flour. He went back to the nest and called again.

"I'm back with leaves and milk for you."

As they always did the rabbits said, "Show us your paw."

This time Bear eagerly showed his flour-covered paw. Since it was white like their mother's the rabbits opened the door. Bear ran in and swallowed them up!

When mother rabbit came back she called out like she always did, "I'm back with leaves and milk for you."

But instead of hearing her children say, "Show us your paw" Bear growled, "Now I'll eat you, too!"

Mother Rabbit was so scared she ran and ran till she met Dog. She told Dog that Bear had eaten her children and Dog walked with her till they met Cat. Rabbit told Cat that Bear had eaten her children and Cat began to walk along with Rabbit and Dog till they met some wasps. Rabbit told the wasps that Bear had eaten her little ones and they joined the rest as they walked along.

After many more animals and insects joined Mother Rabbit, they all walked back to her nest. The wasps went first. They flew inside Rabbit's nest and began stinging Bear so hard and so fast he screamed and ran. And as soon as he was out of the nest the rest of the animals jumped and shoved him down the hill.

When Bear finally stopped rolling Mother Rabbit cut open his stomach, freed her four children and took them back home to their nest.

The Story of Demane and Demazana

*I*n this story collected from the Xhosa people in South Africa, an orphaned brother and sister must protect themselves from a child-eating monster just as Hansel and Gretel must save themselves from the witch. Like other versions of this tale, cleverness and kindness to others prove to be more powerful than brute strength, and the cannibal ends up getting much more than he bargained for!

*O*nce upon a time a brother and sister, who were twins and orphans, were obliged on account of ill usage to run away from their relatives. The boy's name was Demane, the girl's Demazana.

They went to live in a cave that had two holes to let in air and light, the entrance to which was protected by a very strong door, with a fastening inside. Demane went out hunting by day, and told his sister that she was not to roast any meat while he was absent, lest the cannibals should discover their retreat by the smell. The girl would have been quite safe if she had done as her brother commanded. But she was wayward, and one day she took some buffalo meat and put it on a fire to roast.

A cannibal smelt the flesh cooking, and went to the cave, but found the door fastened. So he tried to imitate Demane's voice, and asked to be admitted, singing this song:—

> *Demazana, Demazana,*
> *Child of my mother,*
> *Open this cave to me.*
> *The swallows can enter it.*
> *It has two apertures.*

Demazana said: "No. You are not my brother; your voice is not like his."

The cannibal went away, but after a little time came back again, and spoke in another tone of voice: "Do let me in, my sister."

The girl answered: "Go away, you cannibal; your voice is hoarse, you are not my brother."

So he went away and consulted with another cannibal. He said: "What must I do to obtain what I desire?"

He was afraid to tell what his desire was, lest the other cannibal should want a share of the girl.

His friend said: "You must burn your throat with a hot iron."

He did so, and then no longer spoke hoarse. Again he presented himself before the door of the cave, and sang,—

> *Demazana, Demazana,*
> *Child of my mother,*
> *Open this cave to me.*
> *The swallows can enter it.*
> *It has two apertures.*

The girl was deceived. She believed him to be her brother come back from hunting, so she opened the door. The cannibal went in and seized her.

As she was being carried away, she dropped some ashes here and there along the path. Soon after this, Demane, who had taken nothing that day but a swarm of bees, returned and found his sister gone. He guessed what had happened, and followed the path by means of the ashes until he came to Zim's dwelling. The cannibal's family were [sic] out gathering firewood, but he was at home, and had just put Demazana in a big bag, where he intended to keep her till the fire was made.

Demane said: "Give me water to drink, father."

Zim replied: "I will, if you will promise not to touch my bag."

Demane promised. Then Zim went to get some water; and while he was away, Demane took his sister out of the bag, and put the bees in it, after which they both concealed themselves.

When Zim came with the water, his wife and son and daughter came also with firewood.

He said to his daughter: "There is something nice in the bag; go bring it."

She went, but the bees stung her hand, and she called out: "It is biting."

He sent his son, and afterwards his wife, but the result was the same. Then he became angry, and drove them outside, and having put a block of wood in the doorway, he opened the bag himself. The bees swarmed out and stung his head, particularly his eyes, so that he could not see.

There was a little hole in the thatch, and through this he forced his way. He jumped about, howling in pain. Then he ran and fell headlong into a pond, where his head stuck fast in the mud, and he became a block of wood like the stump of a tree. The bees made their home in the stump, but no one could get their honey, because, when any one tried, his hand stuck fast.

Demane and Demazana then took all Zim's possessions, which were very great, and they became wealthy people.

A Father's Children

"A Father's Children" was collected from a group of people called the Kamba in the eastern area of Africa now called Kenya. It is unusual because it tells of a father who gives birth to three children from his leg! The villain is an eimu, a monstrous ghost of the dead that had been forgotten by the living. Sometimes eimu are men and other times women. All eimu can change their shapes and appearances.

Once long ago four men went hunting and one of them became very ill. His leg grew more and more swollen day after day. When his friends helped him lance the swollen place on his leg they discovered a child growing inside. A head. Two arms. Then a second pair of arms. Then a third. Three children were born from the man's swollen leg—two boys and a girl. The first was named Kathen'ge. The men filled the new father's leg with herbs, and stitched it closed so it would heal. They also mashed food for the babies.

Soon it was time for the men to go home, but the new father had to stay. He knew it was dangerous to remain in the woods because the eimu monster lived near. But it was also dangerous to make his children travel so far while they were still so small.

The man built his children a little tree-hut high in a giant baobab tree. Then he made a rope that stretched from the hut down to the ground.

"Listen," said the father. "When you hear me sing 'Kathen'ge' throw the rope down to me and I'll climb up to see you. But you must not toss it down for anyone else. There are many eimu monsters living near here."

The children agreed. They were growing so fast they could already talk.

The next day the father went hunting. When he returned with meat he called to his children, "Kathen'ge, throw me the rope." They did, and father and children ate well that night safe in their house.

Unknown to them one of the eimu monsters came everyday and listened to the father sing. One day the eimu sang the father's song in hopes of capturing the children. He sang the father's words, but children knew it wasn't their father's voice.

"You must be the eimu," they cried. They threw down a lump of wood that hit him in the face so hard he ran away.

When their father came home the children told him what had happened and he warned them again not to throw down the rope to anyone but him.

The next day the eimu came again and sang the father's song. This time when the children told him to leave they threw a stone that hit him hard on the head.

The eimu was determined to get the children. He went to the man of magic and power and asked for help in changing his voice. The man told him to find a row of marching ants, then lie down and stick out his tongue so all the ants would bite him. The man told him to do this with black ants, too, and then with scorpions. The man promised that after the eimu had been ill for a month he would recover and be able to sing as sweetly as the father did.

A Father's Children

The eimu did exactly as he'd been told. At the end of the month he returned to the baobab tree and sang to the children, "Kathen'ge, throw me the rope."

This time the eimu sounded just like their father and the children happily threw down the rope. As the eimu climbed up the children were surprised at how much weight their father had gained.

"Don't fear," said the eimu in his new sweet voice, "I'm only bringing you lots of meat."

When the eimu finally got up to the hut the children were terrified. He quickly ate all the meat they had, then took them back to his village and ordered them each to weed a field.

Later on when the father returned and saw the dangling rope he knew his children had been taken away. He quickly ran to the man of magic for help.

"Follow the main path," the man advised, "till you find the village of Muvya. An eimu there has your children."

The father ran fast and reached the village by noon. He asked an old woman if she'd seen any children—two boys and a girl. She nodded and pointed to the fields they were weeding.

The father crept near to Kathen'ge, the first-born boy and said, "You're safe. Tonight when the eimu comes and asks for his food, tell him no. Don't worry. I'll be there to kill him."

That evening Kathen'ge thought ahead and dulled the eimu's spear on a stone. The father hid under the monster's bed. All were ready when the eimu came home.

"Children," called the eimu, "Is my supper cooked?"

"No," said Kathen'ge, "I haven't cooked a thing."

"Then death to you!" the eimu yelled. He grabbed his spear and stabbed, but was so dull it wouldn't cut the boy.

"Who ruined my spear?"

"Me!" yelled Kathen'ge. And just as he yelled the father jumped out and shot an arrow in the eimu's eye. Then again and again until he died.

But just before the eimu died he said, "Come cut off my little finger once I am dead. Cut if off and toss it in the fire along with my hut. When you do everything I have ever killed will come back to life."

It was true. People, cattle, and goats. They all returned from the eimu's burning finger. And so the father and his children gathered them up and led them home to their village.

The Grandmother and the Apes

*L*ike "When a Wise Man Dies . . ." this story tells about a child who hides an older relative during a famine. This time the family member in danger is a grandmother, and her granddaughter must outsmart the villainous ape. The tale is from the Baganda people in Uganda, a country in east central Africa northwest of Lake Victoria. As in many African tales, a song plays a vital role.

*L*ong, long ago there was a famine. Many people died of hunger. Many animals died, too, because they could find no grass to eat. Finally the animals began to eat the people. The people were frightened and ran away to another village that was far from the jungle where many of the animals lived.

Now in a village near the jungle there was a family of children who had no father and mother. They lived with their grandfather and grandmother. One day the wild apes caught the old grandfather and ate him. The children were afraid that these apes would eat the grandmother, too, so they took her to a cave and hid her there. Every day they brought her food; in the morning and in the evening. The apes suspected that the grandmother was hiding there in the cave, and they watched and waited for their chance to make her their last meal.

One day, the oldest of the apes came to the house where the children lived. He spoke to the oldest girl, Nakatwe.

"Where is your grandmother," he said.

Nakatwe was frightened and answered, "We do not know where our grandmother is."

The old ape went away. But from then on he watched the children, following them unseen wherever they went. He saw them go to the cave and sing the little song that told the old grandmother they were there:

> *Where will our grandmother be fed?*
> *She will be fed in the little cave.*
> *Grandmother, are you in?"*

"Yes, I am in, my children," the grandmother answered.

Now the old ape heard the song and the answer, and he learned them both by heart. But his voice was gruff and deep. It did not sound like the sweet voice of Nakatwe. Nevertheless, he went to the cave and sang as sweetly as he could:

> *Where will our grandmother be fed?*
> *She will be fed in the little cave.*
> *Grandmother, are you in?*

The grandmother heard the song, but she knew that it was not the voice of Nakatwe. She knew that it was the voice of an old ape. She listened as the old ape sang the song again and again. But she did not go to the door of the cave.

Finally, the old ape went away. He was very angry.

"I will go and see the wise man," he muttered. "He will teach me how to make my voice sound like the voice of Nakatwe."

Soon after he had gone the children came with the evening meal. The grandmother heard them singing a long way off and she was very happy. When she opened the door of the cave and let them in, she cried for joy.

"What is it, grandmother?" they asked. "Why do you cry?" And she told them about the gruff voice that had sung their song.

"It was the oldest ape," they said. "He has watched us and found out where you are."

They told her how the old ape had come to the house in the village and asked for her. They were frightened. But the old grandmother told them not to be troubled.

"I know the sound of his voice," she said. "I will never let him in."

Then the children were afraid that the apes would eat them. Who would bring food to the grandmother in the morning and in the evening if they were eaten? Would the grandmother starve there all alone in the cave?

But the old ape did not want to eat the children. He wanted, very much, to eat the grandmother. Again and again he sang in his gruff voice at the door of the cave. But she never let him in.

One day he went to Omulubale, the wise man who knew the secrets of everything on earth. He gave Omulubale cowrie shells in payment for his advice.

"Please, Omulubale," he said, "tell me how I can make my voice sound like the voice of Nakatwe."

"I know why you want that," said Omulubale. "You want to go to a certain cave and eat an old woman who is hiding there."

The old ape was surprised that Omulubale knew so much. "Yes," he said. "That is why."

"Before I tell you how to gain it I must tell you that the price for this voice is very high," Omulubale said gravely.

But the old ape answered, "Never mind the price. I will pay anything. Tell me what I must do."

Omulubale said, "For two days you must face the sun every morning, very early when it first rises in the east. You must breathe deeply of the fresh morning air. During the whole two days, you must speak to no one, not even to your wife. On the third day, go straight to the cave and speak. Your voice will be like the voice of Nakatwe."

For two days and two nights the old ape followed these directions. Very early on the morning of the third day he went straight to the cave. His voice, when he sang the little song, sounded like the voice of Nakatwe. The old grandmother heard it. She listened very carefully. She was suspicious because it was earlier than the usual time for the children to come. The song was repeated. It sounded exactly like the voice of Nakatwe.

"They have changed the time of coming in order to fool the old ape," she thought. She opened the door of the cave, and the old ape fell upon her and ate her up.

When he had finished, he took the grandmother's clothes and dressed himself in them. He wanted to eat the children, too. Presently the children came.

Nakatwe sang:

Where will our grandmother be fed?
She will be fed in the little cave.
Grandmother, are you in?

Now the old ape knew the verse, but he had forgotten the answer that the grandmother gave. He did not dare to answer.

Again and again Nakatwe sang. There was no answer from the cave. The other children sang with her. But there was only silence from the cave. Finally Nakatwe decided to go back to the village and ask the wise man to tell them what to do. They found Omulubale and Nakatwe said to him:

"Omulubale, the old ape has found out where our grandmother has been hiding. She does not answer us now. I am afraid. Will you tell us what to do?"

Omulubale answered, sadly, "My child, the old ape has found your grandmother and eaten her up."

The children began to cry. Nakatwe cried, too. Then she dried her tears. She said:

"Omulubale, tell me what I can do to punish the old ape for eating our grandmother. He must be punished."

Omulubale answered: "Take this knife. Go to the cave and sing your little song. The old ape is waiting there and he will hear you. He will come to the door and open it.

Nakatwe, be quick and brave. Strike him with the knife. Strike his heart. When he is dead, cut off his right forefinger. If you can do this, your grandmother and all the people of the village whom the apes have eaten will come back."

Nakatwe took the knife. She went to her house and prepared a basket of food. The other children begged her to take them, too, but she would not. She was afraid for them. She took the basket of food and hid the knife in it. Then she went to the cave. She walked very fast. When she came to the cave all was quiet. Nakatwe sang:

> *Where will our grandmother be fed?*
> *She will be fed in the little cave.*
> *Grandmother, are you in?*

The old ape heard her. He did not dare to answer, but he came to the door and opened it. Quickly Nakatwe lifted the knife. She struck the old ape and pierced his heart. When he was dead, she took the knife and cut off his right forefinger. Instantly there in the cave was the old grandmother and all the people of the village whom the apes had eaten.

Singing and shouting they went back to their homes. The men built a new house for Nakatwe and the children and the old grandmother. They drove the apes back, back deep within the jungle. They all lived in peace for many years.

The Three Kids

*T*his tale comes from the Cape Verde Islands, which lie 400 miles off the northwest coast of Africa. Both the language and culture of Cape Verde are heavily influenced by the Portuguese who settled the islands. "Compa" in the story means friend, and "goat-gazelle" means gazelle. "Saib" is a hard word to trace. The "saib" that Wolf goes to for advice might be a type of bird. Whatever it is, it is certainly a creature of special wisdom.

There was a goat-gazelle had three young ones, named Melo, Maria, Sané. She raised them in a house that locked. She came in from the fields to suckle them every day; and she sang,—

> *Melo, Maria, Sané,*
> *Open the door to me to suckle you!*

Wolf heard this song; and he sang with a gruff voice,—

> *Melo, Maria, Sané,*
> *Open the door to me to suckle you!*

"O Sir Wolf! you're not going to get us to eat," they called to him. Wolf went to the *saib'* to ask her how he could make his voice soft like the goat's. "Get a woollen blanket, a pot of water, and a bundle of wood. Make a fire and heat the water. Jump into the pot and tell Nephew to cover it with the blanket. Then your voice will become soft." Wolf staid three days in the pot. Then he went to Goat's house, and sang,—

> *Melo, Maria, Sané,*
> *Open the door to me to suckle you!*

They opened the door, and he swallowed the three of them. He went to the well for a drink. "Sir Wolf," Well asked, "what have you eaten to make you thirsty?"—"I have eaten goose-eggs," answered Wolf.

Goat-Gazelle was going along crying for her children. She met a donkey. Donkey said, "Lady Goat-Gazelle, how is it that every day I meet you singing and dancing, but to-day you are in tears?"—"I have reason to cry, Sir Compa' Donkey; Wolf has eaten up my three little ones."—"Come along with me. I will put Wolf into your hands," said Donkey. When Wolf saw Donkey, he said, "Come here, Compa' Donkey. You are the very one I'm looking for to eat." When Donkey heard this, he ran away. Goat met an ox. Ox said, "Lady Goat-Gazelle, how is that every day I meet you singing and dancing, but to-day you are in tears?"—"I have reason to cry, Sir Compa' Ox; Wolf has eaten up my three little ones."—"Come along with me. I will put Wolf into your hands," said Ox. When Wolf saw Ox, he said, "Come here, you Big-Neck! You are the very one whose blood I would drink." When Ox heard this, he ran away. Goat met a horse. Horse said, "Lady Goat-Gazelle, how is it that every day I meet you singing and dancing, but today you are in tears?"—"I have reason to cry, Sir Compa' Horse; Wolf has eaten up my three little ones."—"Come along with me. I will put Wolf into your hands," said Horse. When Wolf saw Horse, he said, "Come here, Sir Compa' Horse. You are the very one I would wrestle with." Horse made towards Wolf; but when Wolf also advanced, Horse ran away. Goat-Gazelle met an ant. "Lady Goat-Gazelle, how is it that every day I meet you singing and dancing, but to-day you are in tears?"—"I have reason to cry, Coma' Ant; Wolf has eaten up my three little ones."—"Come along with me. I will put Wolf into your hands," said Ant. When Goat-Gazelle saw Ant, she said, "Coma' Ant, I don't think you can hand Wolf over to me. Big fellows like Donkey and Ox and Horse couldn't, how can a little creature like you?" Ant went up to Wolf, and Wolf swallowed her. Ant said, "I am the little ant the smoke of the pipe [*canhot'*] doesn't blacken, the sun of the veranda doesn't burn." She bit a hole in Wolf's entrails. Wolf said, "Ant, let me alone!"—"I won't let you alone until you let out the three sons of Goat-Gazelle." Wolf discharged one. "That's all," he said. "Comadre Ant, I have three sons," said Goat-Gazelle. Ant bit Wolf again. Wolf said, "Ant, let me alone!"—"I won't let you alone until you let out the three sons of Goat-Gazelle." Wolf discharged one. "That's all," he said. "Comadre Ant, I have three sons," said Goat-Gazelle. Ant bit Wolf again. Wolf said, "Ant, let me alone!"—"I won't let you alone until you let out the three sons of Goat-Gazelle." Wolf discharged the last one. Goat-Gazelle took her little ones and went off to the fields.

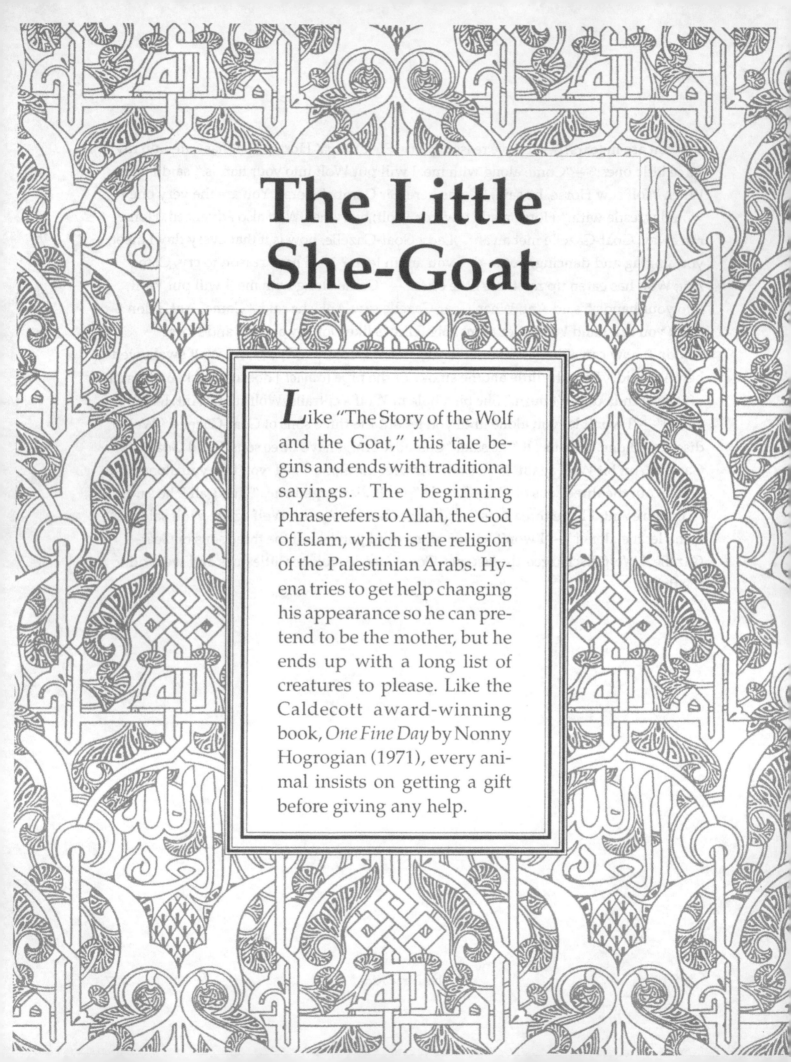

The Little She-Goat

*L*ike "The Story of the Wolf and the Goat," this tale begins and ends with traditional sayings. The beginning phrase refers to Allah, the God of Islam, which is the religion of the Palestinian Arabs. Hyena tries to get help changing his appearance so he can pretend to be the mother, but he ends up with a long list of creatures to please. Like the Caldecott award-winning book, *One Fine Day* by Nonny Hogrogian (1971), every animal insists on getting a gift before giving any help.

Once there was a she-goat who had three kids. She used to say to them, "You stay here. I'm going to bring you some grass." Every day she went grazing until she was full, then she came home with grass for them and said:

O my kids! O my kids!
Open the door for me!
The grass is on my horns
And the milk is in my teats.

They would then open the door for her.

One day the hyena saw her as she was leaving and discovered where her kids were. "By Allah," he said to himself, "I'm going to eat them." Now, the she-goat, before going out, would caution her kids, "If anyone should come and say, 'Let me in,' be careful not to open the door." Because the mother's tail had been chopped off, she said to the kids, "If someone should come and say to you, 'Open for me, I'm your mother,' check first if the tail is chopped off or not. If not, then it can't be me. Don't open the door!"

The hyena went to the cave where the kids were and called out:

O my kids! O my kids!
Open the door for me!
The grass is on my horns
And the milk is in my teats.

"Turn around," they bleated, "and let us see your tail."

Turning around, he displayed his tail, and lo! it was not chopped off.

"Go away!" they said. "You're not our mother."

What was he to do? He wanted to trick them so he could eat them. To the ant he then went and said, "Chop off my tail so I can eat the kids of the little she-goat."

"No," answered the ant, "I won't chop off your tail unless you go to the threshing floor and bring me a measure of wheat."

So to the threshing floor he went and said, "O threshing floor, give me a measure of wheat so I can give it to the ant, and the ant will then chop off my tail so I can eat the kids of the little she-goat."

"I won't give it to you," replied the threshing floor, "unless you bring a team of oxen to tread the wheat on me."

The hyena then went to the oxen and said, "Yoked team, come tread the wheat on the threshing floor, and the threshing floor will give me a measure of wheat, and the measure of wheat I'll give to the ant, and the ant will then chop off my tail so I can eat the kids of the little she-goat."

"We won't go treading," replied the oxen, "unless you tell the spring to give us water to drink."

Going to the pool by the spring, the hyena said, "O pool, let the team of oxen come and drink so that they will tread the wheat on the threshing floor, and the threshing floor will give me a measure of wheat, and the measure of wheat I'll give to the ant, and the ant will then chop off my tail so I can eat the kids of the little she-goat."

"Let the team come and drink," said the pool.

So the team of oxen went and drank at the spring, then they trod the wheat on the threshing floor, and the threshing floor gave a measure of wheat to the ant, and the ant chopped off the hyena's tail.

Back he went to the kids of the little she-goat and called out:

> O my kids! O my kids!
> Open the door for me!
> The grass is on my horns
> And the milk is in my teats.

"Show us your tail," they bleated again.

He showed it to them, and, seeing that it was chopped off, they opened the door for him. In he came and gobbled them all up.

When the little she-goat came home, she discovered the hyena had eaten all her kids. To the blacksmith she then went and said, "Make me iron horns, and make them so sharp I can stab the hyena and get my kids back from his stomach."

The blacksmith made her a pair of iron horns as sharp as knives. The little she-goat put them on, rushed to the house of the hyena, and stomped on the roof.

"Who's pounding on my roof?" roared the hyena. "You've shattered my jars of oil."

"I'm the little she-goat of the twisted horns," announced the goat. "Come on out and let's fight!"

The hyena came out. Piercing him this way and that with her horns, the little she-goat ripped open his stomach and pulled her kids free.

This is my tale, I've told it, and in your hands I leave it.

The Golden Chain from Heaven

This very frightening story from Japan is related to the Chinese and Korean tales in this collection, which feature tigers as the villain. Because Japan has no tigers people there eventually changed the story to include one of their own monsters—Yamauba. Unlike most tales with a knock at the door, this tale ends with a small "pourquoi" tale, which means it explains why something in nature exists or how it came to be.

Very, very long ago, there lived a father and mother and three children. When the youngest child was still small, the father died. On the seventh day after his death, the mother went to visit his grave and left the three children to look after the house.

"In these mountains here, there is a frightful old *yamauba* [malevolent ogress]. While I am gone, even if someone comes, do not open the door," said the mother; then she left.

After a short while the *yamauba* came. "Your mother has returned now," she called out.

"Then put out your hand; let us see," said the children. She stuck out her hand, and they saw that it was covered with hair. "Our mother's hands are much smoother than that. You are a *yamauba*," they said.

The *yamauba* went somewhere, borrowed a razor, and shaved the rough hair off her hand. She took some buckwheat flour and smoothed her hands, then came back to the children's house again. "Your mother has returned now," she called.

"Then let us see your hand," the children said. The *yamauba* stuck out her hand and the children felt of it. It was very nice and smooth, but the *yamauba's* breathing was very rough and her voice sounded like someone rolling kettles down a mountain canyon. "Our mother has a much nicer voice than you," said the boys.

The *yamauba* went and drank some water in which red beans had been washed; then she came back and knocked, *ton ton,* on the door. "Your mother is late, but she has finally returned," she called out.

This time the *yamauba's* voice was just like their mother's, and the boys thought that it must really be she; so they opened the door, and the *yamauba*, disguised as their mother, came into the house.

When they went to bed the two older boys slept in one room as usual, and the youngest boy slept with the disguised *yamauba* mother in an adjoining room. About the middle of the night, as the two older boys were sleeping, they heard a sound, *kori kori,* crunch, crunch, coming from the next room. "Mother, what are you eating?" they called.

"I am eating pickles," replied the *yamauba* mother.

"Please give us one," they begged, and she tore the fingers from one of the child's hands and threw them to the older boys. They picked them up and saw that it was their little brother's fingers; then they realized for the first time that this was the *yamauba*. Softly the two boys got up, took a jar of oil, and left the house. They climbed up in the tree by the gate and poured the oil down the tree trunk.

As soon as the *yamauba* discovered that the two boys had escaped, she ran after them. When she got to the pond by the front gate, she saw the reflection of the boys in the water. She went and got a net and tried to scoop them up out of the water, but she could not do it. By chance she happened to look up and saw the boys up in the tree. She tried to climb up after them, but she kept slipping back down the tree. "How shall I get up in the tree?" she screamed, and the boys became so frightened that they told her to cut notches in the tree. The *yamauba* went to the storeroom and got a sickle. Cutting notches in the tree, she climbed up toward the boys.

The two brothers became so frightened that they didn't know what to do. They prayed, "Deity of the sky, let down an iron chain or something!" Immediately from up in the sky a golden chain descended, *suru suru,* smoothly down to where they were. They grabbed hold of the chain and climbed up it.

When the *yamauba* saw that she prayed, "Deity of the sky, let down a chain or a rope," and immediately a rotten rope came down. The *yamauba* grabbed the rotten rope and started to climb up to the sky, but the rope broke and she fell to the ground.

When she fell her blood gushed out and flowed onto a buckwheat plant that was nearby. It is said that the roots of buckwheat are red now because of what happened then. The brothers climbed on up into the sky; there the older brother became the moon and the younger brother a star.

The Sun and the Moon

*T*his version collected in 1911 has a much longer introduction than most others and tells about the mother's troubles with the tiger before he ever knocks at the door. Its "heavenly" conclusion seems to reflect Korea's long interest in astronomy. Korea built the oldest observatory in the Far East in 647 A.D. Many believe this tale to be the source of the Japanese version, "The Golden Chain from Heaven."

*L*ong, long ago there lived an old woman who had two children, a son and a daughter. One day she went to a neighbouring village to work in a rich man's house. When she left to come back home, she was given a big wooden box containing buckwheat puddings. She carried it on her head, and hastened back to her waiting children. But on the way, as she passed a hill, she met a big tiger.

The tiger blocked her path, and opening its great red mouth asked, "Old woman, old woman! What is that you are carrying on your head?" The old woman replied fearlessly, "Do you mean this, Tiger? It is a box of buckwheat puddings that I was given at the rich man's house where I worked to-day." Then the tiger said, "Old woman, give me one. If you don't, I will eat you up." So she gave the tiger a buckwheat pudding, and it let her pass the hill.

When she came to the next hill the tiger appeared before her and asked her the same question, "Old woman, old woman, what have you got in that box you are carrying on your head?" And, thinking it was another tiger, she gave the same answer, "These are buckwheat puddings I was given at the rich man's house where I worked to-day." The tiger asked for one in the same way. And the old woman gave it a pudding from her box, and it went off into the forest.

The tiger then appeared several more times and made the same demand, and each time she gave it a pudding, until there were no more left in the box. So now she carried the empty box on her head, and she walked along swinging her arms at her sides. Then the tiger appeared again, and demanded a pudding. She explained that she had none left, saying, "Your friends ate all my buckwheat puddings. There is nothing at all left in my box." Thereupon she threw the box away. Then the tiger said, "What are those things swinging at your sides?" "This is my left arm, and this is my right arm," she replied. "Unless you give me one of them, I will eat you up," roared the tiger. So she gave it one of her arms, and it walked off with it. But not long afterwards it appeared in front of her again, and repeated its threats. So she gave it her other arm.

Now the old woman had lost all her puddings, her box, and even both her arms, but she still walked along the mountain road on her two legs. The greedy tiger barred her way once more and asked, "What is that, moving under your body?" She answered, "My legs, of course." The tiger then said, in a rather strange tone, "Oh, in that case, give me one of your legs, or I will eat you up." The old woman got very angry, and complained, "You greedy animal! Your friends ate all my puddings, and both my arms as well. Now you want my legs. However will I be able to get back to my home?" But the tiger would not listen to her, and persisted in its demand. "If you give me your left leg, you can still hop on your right leg, can't you?" So she had to take off her left leg, and throw it to the tiger, and then she set off homewards, hopping on her other leg. The tiger ran ahead of her, and barred her way again. "Old woman, old woman! Why are you hopping like that?" it asked. She shouted furiously, "You devil! You ate all my puddings, both my arms, and one of my legs. However can I go home if I lose my right leg too?" The tiger answered, "You can roll, can't you?" So she cut off her right leg, and gave it to the tiger. She set out to roll over and over along the road. Then the tiger rushed after her, and swallowed what was left of her in a single gulp.

Back at the old woman's home her two children waited till nightfall for her to return. Then they went inside and locked the door, and lay down hungry on the floor, for they did not know that a tiger had eaten their mother on her way home.

The cunning tiger dressed in the old woman's clothes, and put a white handkerchief on its head. Then, standing erect on its hind legs, it walked to the old woman's house and knocked at the door. It called to the two children, "My dears, you must be very hungry. Open the door. I have brought you some buckwheat puddings." But the children remembered the advice their mother had given them when she went out in the morning, "There are tigers about. Be very careful." They noticed that the voice sounded rather strange, and so they did not open the door, and said, "Mother, your voice sounds rather strange. What has happened to you?" So the tiger disguised its voice and said, "Don't be alarmed. Mother is back. I have spent the day spreading barley to dry on mats, and the sparrows kept flying down to eat it, so that I had to shout loudly at them all day long to drive them away. So I have got rather hoarse." The children were not convinced, and asked again, "Then, Mother, please put your arm in through the hole in the door, and let us see it." The tiger put one of its forepaws in the hole in the door. The children touched it and said, "Mother, why is your arm so rough and hairy?" So the tiger explained, "I was washing clothes, and I starched them with rice paste. That must have made my arm rough." But the children peeped out through the hole in the door, and were surprised to see a tiger there in the darkness. So they slipped quietly out the back door, and climbed a tall tree and hid among the branches.

The tiger waited for a while, but as it got no further reply from inside, it broke into the house, and searched in vain for the children. It came out in a furious temper, and rushed round the house with terrible roars, till it came to an old well underneath the tree. It looked down at the water, and there saw the reflections of the two children. So it forced a smile and tried to scoop up the reflections, and said in a gentle voice, "Oh, my poor children. You have fallen into the well. I haven't got a bamboo basket, or even a grass one. How can I save you?" The children watched the tiger's antics from above, and could not help bursting out laughing. Hearing their laughter it looked up, and saw them high in the tree. It asked in a kindly voice, "How did you get up there? That's very dangerous. You might fall into the well. I must get you down. Tell me how you got up so high." The children replied, "Go to the neighbours and get some sesame oil. Smear it on the trunk and climb up."

So the stupid tiger went to the house next door and got some sesame oil and smeared it thickly on the trunk and tried to climb up. But of course the oil made the tree very slippery. So the tiger asked again, "My dear children. You are very clever, aren't you? However did you get up there so easily, right to the top? Tell me the truth." This time they answered innocently, "Go and borrow an axe from the neighbours. Then you can cut footholds on the trunk." So the tiger went and borrowed an axe from the house next door, and, cutting steps in the tree, began to climb up.

The children now thought that they would not be able to escape from the tiger, and in great terror prayed to the God of Heaven. "Oh God, please save us. If you are willing, please send us the Heavenly Iron Chain. But if you mean us to die, send down the Rotten Straw Rope!" At once a strong Iron Chain came gently down from Heaven to them, so that they could climb up without difficulty.

When the tiger reached the top of the tree the children were gone. It wanted to follow them, so it too began to pray, but in opposite terms, because it was very afraid that it might be punished for its misdeeds. "Oh God of Heaven, if you would save me, send down the Rotten Straw Rope, I beg of you. But if you mean me to die, please send down the Heavenly Iron Chain." By praying in this way, it hoped that the Iron Chain would come down, and not the Straw Rope, for it expected that as a punishment it would receive the opposite of what it had prayed for. But the gods are straightforward, and always willing to save lives by answering prayers directly, and so it was the Rotten Straw Rope that came down after all. The tiger seized the rope, and began to climb up it, for in the darkness it could not see that it was not the chain. When it got a little way up the rope broke, and so it fell down to the ground. It crashed down in a field of broom-corn, where it died crushed and broken, its body pierced through by the sharp stems of the corn. From that day, it is said, the leaves of broom-corn have been covered with blood red spots.

The two children lived peacefully in the Heavenly Kingdom, until one day the Heavenly King said to them, "We do not allow anyone to sit here and idle away the time. So I have decided on duties for you. The boy shall be the Sun, to light the world of men, and the girl shall be the moon, to shine by night." Then the girl answered, "Oh King, I am not familiar with the night. It would be better for me not to be the moon." So the King made her the Sun instead, and made her brother the moon.

It is said that when she became the Sun people used to gaze up at her in the sky. But she was a modest girl, and greatly embarrassed by this. So she shone brighter and brighter, so that it was impossible to look at her directly. And that is why the sun is so bright, that her womanly modesty might be for ever respected.

The Sun and the Moon

The Lame Wolf

*T*his tale from the western area of India, the state of Rajasthan, is different from other versions in two major ways. It begins before the children are born, telling how the mother deer builds their house and gets their food. Two of the foods she gets are familiar to North Americans though not by their Indian names. *Jaggery* is a kind of brown sugar and *ghee* is a type of butter. The story also includes a magic tree that helps the children much like a fairy godmother would.

Once there was a deer. She was carrying four little ones and so when she moved about she would soon feel fatigued. Often, she lay down on the forest path to rest. One day, a cart full of hay came up. The cartdriver, seeing the deer lying in the way, stopped and said, "Keep off the path, deer. My bullocks are excitable and may gore you to death." The deer did not give him room to go, but said, "Brother, I am an expectant mother. If I give birth to my little ones in the open they will die of cold; other animals will devour them. But if you give me this cartload of hay I could build myself a hut. Help your sister and she will pray that you and your children prosper."

How could the cartdriver ignore this request? He took the cart up to the place that the deer had selected for her hut, and emptied his load there. The deer made her hut near a saffron tree and then again went and lay down on the pathway.

After a while a man came with a cart loaded with doors. Seeing the deer, he too stopped and said, "Keep off the path, deer, my bullocks are excitable and may gore you to death." Again the deer did not move and said, "Brother, I am an expectant mother and I need your help. Before you, there came a cartdriver who gave me a stack of hay to build myself a hut, but it has no doors and if I litter there, my young ones will surely be devoured by some beast. Give a pair of doors to your sister and she will pray that you and your children multiply and prosper."

The cartdriver's heart filled with pity for the poor creature and he agreed to carry a pair of doors to her hut. The deer fixed the doors, shut them fast and again lay down in her usual place. Soon another cartman came that way. He was carrying rice and jaggery and he too called out, "Keep off the path, deer. My bullocks are excitable and may gore you to death." And the deer requested him too, to help her. "Brother," she said, "I am an expectant mother. One cartdriver gave me a stack of hay to make my hut, another a pair of doors. If I had jaggery and rice, I could plaster the walls and the floor. Will you not help your sister that she may bless you so that you and your children multiply and prosper." The cartdriver was touched by the plea of the innocent deer and emptied the cart at her doorstep. The deer plastered the walls and the floor and again came to the usual spot.

Another cartdriver now reined his bullocks to a stop. He was carrying sugar, ghee, dried ginger, gum and aniseed. He tried to shoo the deer off the path and said, "Quick, make way for my cart. My bullocks are excitable and may gore you to death." The deer, however, did not budge, and said, "Brother, I am an expectant mother. Before you there

The Lame Wolf

came a cartdriver who gave me a stack of hay to build myself a hut, another gave me a pair of doors, and yet another, rice and jaggery to plaster the walls and floor. Could you not spare some of the things you carry, for they are eaten by young mothers after confinement. Help your sister and your little nephews will pray that you and your children prosper."

The cartdriver had not the heart to turn down the request of an expectant mother and the deer got what she wanted. She profusely thanked the cartdriver and after he had gone she prepared and stored the special food eaten by young mothers. Soon after, four pretty deer were born to her. She tenderly nursed them and herself fed on the food that she had stored. For forty days she did not move out of the hut, but after that when she had bathed and worshipped the sun-god and performed the conventional ceremonies, she came out.

Now she would everyday go to graze in the forest. And always while leaving, she cautioned the children never to open the door in her absence. When she would return home in the evening, she would stand by the door and say:

> *My sweet little ones,*
> *In the hut plastered with jaggery*
> *And decorated with rice,*
> *Open the door for your mother.*

Then the children at once opened the door and as soon as they saw their mother, they clamored to be near her and clung to her. And the joy of the mother deer knew no bounds.

In this same forest there lived a lame wolf. He was addicted to eating the tender flesh of the little ones of animals. He had his eye on the deer's young ones. One day he went to the hut and knocked at the door. "Who is there?" shouted the children. In reply the wolf knocked again. The children guessed that it was not their mother. She had instructed them not to open the door unless they heard the words:

> *My sweet little ones,*
> *In the hut plastered with jaggery*
> *And decorated with rice,*
> *Open the door for your mother.*

The lame wolf tried all his tricks but failed to get the door opened. Disappointed and angry he returned home. In the evening he came again and hid behind some bushes. Having heard what transpired between the mother and children, he tiptoed away. The next morning he returned to the hut and mimicking the deer said:

> *My sweet little ones,*
> *In the hut plastered with jaggery*
> *And decorated with rice,*
> *Open the door for your mother.*

The children jumped for joy and rushed to the door, but the saffron tree warned them, "Stop! It is the lame wolf. Don't open the door." The wolf was furious and he pulled the saffron tree out by its roots.

After some time he again said:

> *My sweet little ones,*
> *In the hut plastered with jaggery*
> *And decorated with rice,*
> *Open the door for your mother.*

But again the uprooted saffron tree lying on the ground groaned, "Stop! Don't open the door. It is the lame wolf." In desperation the wolf burnt the saffron tree and mixing the ashes with water gulped them down.

After a while he again imitated the deer:

> *My sweet little ones,*
> *In the hut plastered with jaggery*
> *And decorated with rice,*
> *Open the door for your mother.*

The children waited—if it was the lame wolf again, surely the saffron tree would warn them. No, it must be their mother. They unlatched the door and happily crowded forward—then stopped suddenly, a terrified lot. There they stood face to face with the greedy wolf. In no time he had devoured his prey and slunk back to his lair.

In the evening when the deer returned home she found the door wide open. Outside the hut were marks of the wolf's feet. The saffron tree was nowhere to be seen. She felt dizzy. She ran into the hut. Her forebodings were true. It was empty! She burst into tears and with loud lamentations, she followed the wolf's tracks. These led her to the banks of a lake and there she espied him as he, belching with satisfaction, walked down to the edge of the water to have a drink. The deer wiped her tears and said, "O cruel wolf, give me back my children."

The wolf's eyes gleamed as he spoke, "What do I know of your children. Am I their keeper?" And he moved his foreleg over his stomach and belched loudly. The deer again burst into tears and cried, "May you perish lame wolf, for you have devoured my little ones!"

But the wolf hardly cared for such curses. He calmly lowered his head to drink water while she, weeping bitterly, prayed, "May the one who devoured my little ones become blind." and sure enough, the wolf, as he stood drinking water, was suddenly blinded. He roared angrily and tried to spring upon the deer, but she swiftly bounded aside and again cursed him, "May the one who devoured my children break his legs." And the wolf as he ran stumbled and fell and broke his legs. While he roared louder, the deer said, "May his stomach burst, for he has devoured my children." *Phut!* His stomach burst open and out popped the four frisking, pretty young deer and a fresh green saffron sapling.

The children ran to their mother's side. "We are hungry," they clamored. The deer bathed and fed them and brought them back home. She carried the saffron sapling and planted it in its old place near the hut. And now everyday she waters it with sweetened milk and her children feed on milk flavoured with its flowers.

As for the wolf, he lay there by the side of the lake and kites and crows feasted on his remains.

The Monkey and the Hyena

*T*his tale comes from the Ngoni people of Malawi, a country in southeast Africa. Extended families are highly honored among the peoples of Malawi. Relatives often watch after other relatives as the heroic monkey does in this tale. Like the tale from Cameroon, "When a Wise Man Dies . . . ," the villain in this version must call for a rope to be dropped rather than knock at a door. Here the rope is a woody vine called a *liana*.

Chatter, chatter, chatter went the little tree Monkeys in the cool depths of the forest—cool, even though the sun was shining fiercely; dark even though the day was bright. For the trees of the forest were great with age and their branches interlaced and intertwined in a conspiracy to shut out all light. It was like being in a vast cathedral; like living in perpetual twilight; like moving in some great cavern of the sea where all things swam in dim veridian mystery.

Strange things grew there: ferns, orchids, creepers. Strange things lived there and never was there silence. All day long the Monkeys chattered, and the Turacos screeched, and at night the Owls hooted and every bush gave forth some secret rustle.

The Monkeys lived happily enough. They had a fine time, swinging through the treetops; sliding down the giant lianas that hung from almost every branch; pulling each other's tails. There was no end to their pranks and games. Only when the voice of an enemy could be heard did they pause in their play until they remembered that really they were quite safe, for what enemy could reach them? Who could climb so high? Certainly not Fisi, the Hyena, who was the greatest enemy they had!

Chatter, chatter, chatter! The Monkeys were getting ready for a party. They were going to visit another colony of Monkeys who lived on the far side of the forest. Not all of them, of course. The smallest babies could not go and someone had to stay behind to look after them. Who should that someone be?

"Nyonyo shall stay," said the Oldest-and-most-Important Monkey, severely.

"Why should it be me?" demanded an indignant young voice.

"Because you had the impertinence to throw a bush-orange at me this morning, and . . ."

"Oh, it wasn't at you," Nyonyo burst out. "You know it was meant for Pusi!"

"Silence! How dare you argue with me. In any case, I won't have you throwing things at my dear Pusi." And the old Monkey looked fondly at her son, who was a tiresome little wretch, disliked by almost every Monkey in the colony.

"Now, Nyonyo, mind you take good care of the babies, and let this be a lesson to you." With a magnificent gesture she gave the starting signal, and in a minute all the Monkeys, except Nyonyo and his charges, were swinging away gaily through the treetops at a tremendous pace.

Nyonyo made a grimace at their retreating forms and sat down and sighed.

"Well," said he to himself, "I'm sorry that bush-orange missed young Pusi but I'm glad now that it hit the old lady. It hit her hard, too!" And Nyonyo began to chuckle heartily at the recollection of the morning's episode.

He was still chuckling when a voice hailed him from below.

"Hey! You little Monkey up there," it said. "You who are laughing so merrily. I want to join you. I want to come and play with you. If I hold on to this liana will you pull me up?"

Nyonyo stopped laughing and peered down through the dim green light. The underbrush was very thick down there and he could see nothing.

"Who are you?" he asked. There was just a shade of suspicion in his voice, for the voice below was harsh and gruff.

"A friend. Pull me up, little Monkey. I do so want to come and play with you."

"What's your name?" demanded Nyonyo again. He was getting more and more suspicious every moment.

"Come on, pull me up!" said the wheedling voice.

Again Nyonyo peered down into the undergrowth. Was that an ugly great paw grasping the liana? He couldn't be sure, but quite suddenly he was absolutely certain whose was the ugly harsh voice.

"Pull me up quickly!"

"No, oh no, Fisi. I know you. I know your gruff, snarly voice. You don't want to play with me. You want to eat me for dinner. I know you!"

"What nonsense!" said the Hyena in the silkiest tones he could produce. "Of course I wouldn't do such a thing. I just want a game of catch."

"Yes, I know your sort of 'catch,' but I've no intention of being caught! Go away, Fisi, go away!" And the little Monkey seized a twig and threw it at the Hyena.

"Grrr!" growled Fisi, furiously. "I'll pay you out for that. I'll have you for dinner one of these days!"

"Well, you'll have to be a lot cleverer than you are at present," Nyonyo retorted cheerfully, throwing down another twig. He was rather pleased with himself for not having been taken in and he felt quite safe up on his high branch. But he knew he'd feel still safer if Fisi would only go away.

After a few more growls and threats Fisi went. He went straight to his friends, the White Ants, for he wanted advice and the White Ants were very clever. There was

The Monkey and the Hyena

nothing they didn't know. How could he make his voice sweet and gentle, he asked? Well, it wouldn't be easy, they replied, but if he rubbed his vocal cords with honey every night and every morning, his voice would undoubtedly improve. Could they let him have some honey? He didn't like to ask the Bees because he wasn't very friendly with Bees! Yes, the Ants would get some honey for him and he should have it on the morrow.

Fisi thanked them very much indeed and went back to his home in a fever of impatience. He longed to try the honey at once. If only it would sweeten his voice. If only it would be successful. Then he'd be able to deal with that Monkey!

A week passed. Twice every day Fisi had rubbed his vocal cords with honey and hundreds of times a day he had tried talking sweetly, softly, gently to himself. Sometimes he even went to the White Ants and said in a queer sort of husky, sticky, eager voice: "Don't you think my voice is sweet now?" And the White Ants would reply evasively: "It certainly is improving. It is much less harsh."

On the eighth day of treatment Fisi decided that he could wait no longer, so he went to the Monkey's tree and called out as gently as he could:

"Hey! Little Monkey! I've come to play with you. I've got a nice surprise for you. I'll hold on to this liana and you can pull me up."

Now it so happened that Nyonyo was again in charge of the baby Monkeys, for he had again got into disfavour with the Important Old Lady; and at that moment there was nothing he wanted so much as someone to play with. What luck that someone had come along! He was just going to pull up the liana when it occurred to him that he did not know who the someone was. The voice was not one he recognised.

"Who are you?" he asked.

"A friend," replied Fisi.

"Yes, but who? And what's wrong with your voice? It sounds sort of sticky and husky."

"There's nothing wrong with my voice," answered Fisi indignantly and much less softly.

"Isn't there, though?" Nyonyo sat bolt upright. That last remark had had a familiar harshness in it. It was nearly as harsh as Fisi's voice. Could it be Fisi himself? Could it? Well, he'd give a little pull at the liana and if the person at the other end was very heavy, Nyonyo would know that it *was* Fisi.

He gave a sharp tug. The weight on the liana was tremendous. If it wasn't Fisi down there it was someone just as heavy and none of the other big animals ever came to call on the Monkeys. It must be Fisi! Nyonyo hurriedly let go of the liana.

"Ow!" yelled the Hyena, as he fell to the ground with a bump (and the harshness in his voice was very noticeable).

"You stupid little Monkey! What did you do that for? Come on, pull me up properly!"

"Oh, no, Fisi! I know you now. I know your voice and no one else could be so heavy. You'll have to be a lot cleverer before you can catch me. Go away, Fisi!" And Nyonyo threw down a twig which caught the Hyena squarely on the nose and made him let out another sharp "Ow!"

Fuming with rage and disappointment, Fisi stalked off and again went to see the White Ants. "How could he get his weight down?" he wanted to know. "By eating much less," the White Ants told him, which did not comfort him at all. But all that week Fisi *did* eat less and every night and every morning he still rubbed honey on his vocal cords. And on the eighth day he went again to the Monkey's tree and called out ever so softly, oh, so sweetly:

"Hey! You little Monkeys! Here's a kind friend come to see you. Quickly pull me up on the liana."

Now although some of the Monkeys were away visiting elsewhere in the forest, on this occasion both Nyonyo and Pusi were amongst those who had stayed behind, and it was Pusi who heard the soft, sweet voice.

"Who are you?" he asked.

"A friend. A kind friend who has got a lovely surprise for you."

"Ooh!" exclaimed Pusi excitedly. "Have you got a present for me?"

"Yes, of course I have. Pull me up quickly and you'll see."

"Come on, then," said Pusi and began to haul on the liana with all his might. "You do weight a lot," he grumbled after a few seconds, and called to Nyonyo to come and help.

"Why do you want help?" asked Nyonyo.

"There's a friend down below with a present for me and he's very heavy."

"Who is it?"

"I don't know. Come and help when I tell you to!"

"Oho!" said Nyonyo. "Why should I do what *you* tell me? Just you find out who your friend is and then perhaps I'll come and help. It may be an enemy for all you know. It may be Fisi, the Hyena."

"As if I don't know Fisi's voice!" exclaimed Pusi, scornfully. "This is a sweet, soft voice, so don't be stupid. If you don't come and help at once I'll call my mother."

"I'm not going to pull up that liana until I know who is on it," said Nyonyo obstinately.

"Mamma! Mamma!" called out Pusi. "Nyonyo won't help me with this liana. He's jealous because there's a friend below who is bringing me a present."

"Go help my little Pusi at once," ordered the Important Old Monkey.

"Not till I know who is down there," answered Nyonyo. "It may be Fisi!"

"Do you think my clever little Pusi doesn't know the voice of Fisi, the Hyena?" demanded the old lady shrilly as she swung down on to Nyonyo's branch and began to box his ears. But Nyonyo was too quick for her. He curled his tail round the branch and slid beneath, and the old lady, muttering angrily, went to help her son pull up the liana.

They pulled and they pulled, and Nyonyo still hung by his tail from the branch. Slowly the liana came up until, even in the dim twilight of the forest, Nyonyo could make out the large, ugly form of Fisi. The Hyena was clutching the liana tightly and on his face was an evil smirk of triumph.

"Let go," shouted Nyonyo in a panic. "It *is* Fisi! Let go that liana or he will eat us all!"

But Pusi and his mother took no notice. They simply went on hauling steadily and Fisi was already more than halfway up.

Desperately Nyonyo swung himself at the liana, grasped it in his paws and started to bite. It was very thick. Could he possibly bite through it in time?

Nearer and nearer came Fisi, smirking wickedly and licking his lips. Suddenly he realised what Nyonyo was trying to do.

"Here! Stop that!" he yelled. "Stop . . ." and at that moment the liana broke. With a tremendous crash, Fisi fell howling to the ground.

From every part of the tree Monkeys came hurrying, chattering with excitement, wanting to know what had happened. Nyonyo told them.

"Well done, Nyonyo!" they cried, "Well done! You have saved us all! Now *you* shall be our Leader."

Journey to the Mending City

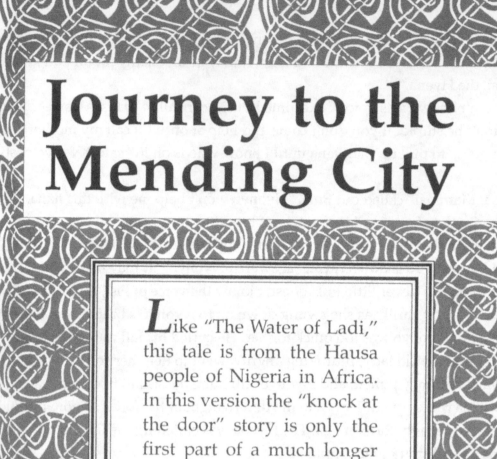

*L*ike "The Water of Ladi," this tale is from the Hausa people of Nigeria in Africa. In this version the "knock at the door" story is only the first part of a much longer tale. In the past, Hausa custom allowed men to marry more than one woman, and this tale has two wives. After the kind wife saves her child, a second wife greedily tries to improve *her* daughter's life by copying the first mother's actions. "Mother Holle," collected by the Brothers Grimm, has a similar plot.

*O*nce long ago all the young women of a village were gathering herbs in the forest when it began to rain. They ran for safety in the hollow of a baobab tree, but only found more trouble. As soon as they were inside the tree the Devil sealed it up. He said he would only let them go if they gave him their cloth and necklaces. All but one young woman agreed. She was left in the tree while the others went home.

When the girl's mother heard what happened she went to the tree and searched till she found a small hole in the top. That evening she took food to the girl and called,

> *Daughter, dear daughter,*
> *Reach through the hole.*
> *I've brought some food for you.*

The daughter reached for the food and the mother went home. What neither the mother or daughter knew was a hyena had heard everything. He went to the tree and called the same words.

> *Daughter, dear daughter,*
> *Reach through the hole.*
> *I've brought some food for you.*

The girl refused. "Your voice is not my mother's voice."

The hyena was determined to catch the girl. He went to the blacksmith and ordered, "Change my voice to a human's voice."

The blacksmith agreed. "But I know you'll eat the first thing you see long before you get to the tree and ruin your voice."

That's just what happened. Hyena saw a centipede on his way to the tree and ate it. When he got to the tree and called out the words the girl refused to reach through the hole.

"No. Your voice is not my mother's voice."

Hyena ran back to the blacksmith and threatened to eat him because he hadn't properly changed his voice. Afraid for his life the blacksmith agreed to change hyena's voice to always sound like a human's voice.

This time when hyena called,

> *Daughter, dear daughter,*
> *Reach through the hole,*
> *I've brought some food for you*

he sounded just like the girl's mother. The girl reached through the hole, but before she could even call for help he grabbed her hand, pulled her out and ate her all except for the bones.

When the mother brought food that evening all she found was her daughter's bones. She cried till she could cry no more. Then she got a basket, gathered all the bones and headed for the city where people are mended. As she walked she came to a place where some food was cooking itself.

"Food," she asked. "Can you show me the way to the city where people are mended?"

"Stay here," said the food. "Eat me instead."

The mother said thanks, but she had no appetite and didn't want to eat.

"Then," said the food, "when you have gone so far take the road to the right and not the one to the left."

The mother walked on and came to a place where more food was cooking itself.

"Food," she asked. "Can you show me the way to the city where people are mended?"

"Stay here," said the food. "Eat me instead."

The mother said thanks, but she had no appetite and didn't want to eat.

"Then," said the food, "when you have gone so far take the road to the right and not the one to the left."

The mother kept walking and walking and came to a place where more food was cooking itself.

"Food," she asked. "Can you show me the way to the city where people are mended?"

"Stay here," said the food. "Eat me instead."

Once again the mother said thanks, but she had no appetite and didn't want to eat.

"Then," said the food, "when you have gone so far take the road to the right and not the one to the left."

At last she reached the city where people are mended. She told them hyena had eaten her child and gave them the basket of her daughter's bones.

"Yes," said the people. "Your daughter will be mended soon."

The next morning at dawn they told the mother to take the cattle out to feed for the day. The only food for the cattle was the fruit of the Adduwa tree and the mother picked all the fruit she could. She only ate the green ones herself and gave the cattle the best.

That night when she brought the cattle home the biggest bull called out for all to hear, "This woman has a beautiful heart. Her daughter must be mended well."

And she was. The next day the mother and daughter started home as healthy and beautiful as she'd ever been.

Now it happened that the people of the woman's village accepted men having more than one wife. The mother of the girl newly mended had a rival wife who also had a daughter. This woman's daughter was as ugly as the other was lovely. The rival wife decided to do the same as the first wife and have her daughter mended to be better than before.

The rival mother put her daughter in a mortar and began to pound her up. The daughter resisted, but the mother kept pounding down to the bones. Then she put all the bones in a basket and headed for the city where people are mended.

As she walked she came to the place where some food was cooking itself.

"Food," she asked. "Can you show me the way to the city where people are mended?"

"Stay here," said the food. "Eat me instead."

The rival mother gladly ate every bit of the food. A while later she came to the second place where some food was cooking itself.

"Food," she asked. "Can you show me the way to the city where people are mended?"

"Stay here," said the food. "Eat me instead."

The rival mother gladly ate every bit of the food. She kept on walking and eventually came to the third place where some food was cooking itself.

"Food," she asked. "Can you show me the way to the city where people are mended?"

"Stay here," said the food. "Eat me instead."

The rival mother happily ate a third time.

In time she reached the city where people are mended. When the people asked her why she had come she told a lie.

"Hyena has eaten my daughter. Here are her bones."

Just as before the people took the basket and said, "Your daughter will be mended soon."

The next morning at dawn they told the rival mother to take the cattle out to feed for the day. As she picked the fruits off the Adduwa tree she ate the sweetest ones herself and left green ones on the ground for the cattle.

When she returned that night with the cattle the biggest bull called out for all to hear, "This woman has a greedy heart. Her daughter can't be mended well."

And she was not. When the second girl was mended she was only half of who she had been. One leg, one hand, half nose. Only half of who she had been.

When the mother and daughter started home the next day the mother ran off and hid in the grass.

"Mother," called the daughter, "it's time to go."

But the mother resisted. "Go away. You're not my child."

"But mother," said the daughter, "you are mine."

They walked a while longer and again the mother ran off, this time to hide by a tree. Just as before the daughter followed her mother's footprints.

"Mother," she called, "it's time to go."

The mother resisted. "Go away. Go away. You're not my child."

But mother," said the daughter, "you are mine."

They walked a while longer, then the mother ran off and hid in a cave.

"Mother," called the daughter, "it's time to go."

Again she resisted. "Go away. Go away! You're not my child."

"But mother," said the daughter, "you are mine."

Once more they started off and as soon as they reached their village the mother ran to their hut and shut the door.

"Mother," called the daughter, "I've come back home."

The mother wouldn't speak or open the door. But the daughter called out again and again, then pulled the door open.

"Mother of mine. I've come back home."

And so they lived from that day on with the mother always having to see what she'd done to her daughter.

Indesoka

This tale comes from Madagascar, a large island off the southeast coast of Africa. The island's lack of large carnivorous animals such as wolves and bears may be one reason this version has a human cannibal as the villain. The story is rather violent. Like many women in folktales, the mother in this tale has strong inner resources and uses her cleverness to save her daughter and punish the villain. It was the custom in older times—like in this tale—for both men and women to plait, or braid, their hair.

*O*ne day when Indesoka was to meet her friends at the river she was late and made a mistake. Instead of taking the old clay pot she grabbed her father's silver vessel. When she got to the river all her friends said, "Look, we've broken our water pots. Break yours, too, then none us will get in trouble."

Indesoka agreed and hit hers against a stone, but since it was silver instead of clay it didn't break.

Her friends said, "Try again. Try again."

Indesoka was afraid her father, an ogre, would be very mad, but she still did what her friends all wanted her to do. She took a stone and hammered her vessel again and again till it was finally broken. But as soon as it was broken, her friends all laughed and pulled out their pots from their hiding place. They hadn't broken their pots at all!

Indesoka was so upset she ran to a cave that was blocked with stones. "If I am loved," she called, "open up, let me in." It did. And when she called again the stones closed the cave behind her.

When the other girls returned to the village they told Indesoka's father that she had broken his silver vessel. He got so angry he roared and screamed, "I'll kill her and eat her myself!"

He told his wife to take Indesoka's supper to her. "Bring her home," he lied, "I really don't mean to eat her."

When Indesoka's mother reached the cave she sang a song:

> *Indesoka Indesoka*
> *Hidden in the cave*
> *Indesoka Indesoka*
> *Friends have deceived you*
> *Now your father wants you dead*
> *Indesoka Indesoka*
> *Here's your rice and meat*

Indesoka was so glad to hear her mother's voice she sang her song that opened the cave. Once she had eaten she told her mother goodbye and sang to close the cave again.

When Indesoka's mother returned home she said, "I wasn't able to find the cave. I ate the food myself."

The next day when the rice and meat were cooked Indesoka's angry father took the food to the cave himself and sang the mother's song.

Indesoka Indesoka
Hidden in the cave
Indesoka Indesoka
Friends have deceived you
Now your father wants you dead
Indesoka Indesoka
Here's your rice and meat

Indesoka knew the harsh voice was her father's voice and didn't say a word. Even madder than before her father asked the heavens what to do next. The oracle replied, "Drink a raw egg and your voice will soften to sound like your wife's."

The next time he sang to the cave he sounded just like his wife.

Indesoka Indesoka
Hidden in the cave
Indesoka Indesoka
Friends have deceived you
Now your father wants you dead
Indesoka Indesoka
Here's your rice and meat

Certain it was her mother's voice, Indesoka sang her song to open the cave. But as soon as it was open her father killed and butchered her, all for a broken vessel.

When he got home he lied to his wife. "Here's her food. I couldn't find her either, but I did catch this lamb for us to eat."

As soon as the mother looked at the meat she knew what had happened and began to cry, "My child, my child."

The ogre yelled, "What?"

"Nothing," said the mother. "I only wish my Indesoka could taste this lamb."

She cooked it like the ogre ordered her to do and invited everyone to eat. She cried as she worked, but dared not stop for fear of what the ogre would do.

Everyone came and ate as the ogre told them to do. Then as soon as they were done Indesoka's mother collected all her bones and set them in the sun to dry.

When Indesoka's bones were dry her mother pounded them to dust and put them in a clean vessel. Then she put that vessel inside a basket, then that basket in another basket six times more. Before long the bones began to join together again. Then

Indesoka's head began to appear. Slowly the rest of her body came out and finally her hands and feet. She looked exactly like she did before.

When her ogre-father saw her again Indesoka's mother quickly lied. "No. She only looks like my child. You've eaten Indesoka. This girl is my sister's child."

"I see," said the ogre. "Come plait my hair."

"Of course," said his wife. "Come here by the post."

Indesoka's mother worked quickly to braid the ogre's long hair. As she did she braided it and tied it tight around the post.

When he started to fuss she said, "Just a bit. I'm almost done."

As soon as she was done Indesoka's mother stared and said, "You killed my daughter. Your life is done!"

The ogre tried to get away but his hair was braided to the post. His wife took the same knife he'd used to kill Indesoka and stuck him and stuck till he was dead. After that she cleaned the flesh from the bones, pounded it, salted it, and sent it to all his relatives as a gift to eat. After everyone had eaten some she told them what she'd done.

Indesoka was safe again, and as their local custom ruled, she and her mother inherited all her father's land and wealth.

Indesoka

The Tiger Witch

*T*he Tiger Witch in this tale lives in a house made of sweets much as the witch does in "Hansel and Gretel." This variant was collected on the island of Taiwan, a Chinese-speaking country off the southeastern coast of China. Though traditional culture did not view women as equal to men this tale features two very clever and heroic girls. This tale is a cousin to the story told in Ed Young's Caldecott award-winning book, *Lon Po Po* (1989).

Near Alishan in Taiwan, there was said to be a woman who was really a Tiger Witch. Some said she lived in a house made of sugar cane and candied sweet oranges, and that she lured little children inside it with gifts of sweet potatoes and such goodies.

Once inside, the children would be dipped in tempura batter and fried a crisp brown. Then the Tiger Witch would eat them and save the bones, which she dropped into her pocket for between meal snacks, crunching them like peanuts. She was said to be especially fond of finger bones.

Everyone knew about her. Dreadful stories of her wicked behavior sifted through the bamboo thicket that surrounded the village where Ah-lee and Ah-bi lived with their mother and father and their baby brother. For safety, every house had a *baqua* eye painted on wood or paper hanging on the door post to keep witches and demons from crossing the threshold, so the two sisters never worried about the tales of the Tiger Witch.

One day the father of the family went on a journey to the sea with the magistrate of the district. He was gone for many days, and finally the mother, in her concern, decided to go to the temple in the next village to make a sacrifice of pork and chicken to the gods there, who were noted for bringing travelers home safely.

"Shut the door tightly and don't let anyone in the house until I come back," warned the mother. "I shall stay overnight, for I must stop to visit my own mother while I am near my old home. If anything bothers you, run tell the old priest in the temple across the rice paddy."

The mother strapped the baby onto her back, put the port and chicken into her bag, and set out.

It was a long and lonely day for Ah-bi and Ah-lee, for they lived in a remote house in the middle of a rice paddy on the edge of the village near the old Taoist temple.

Late in the afternoon the girls sat on the doorstep of the house, listening to the temple bells while they ate their rice and drank their tea. Ah-bi put down her chopsticks and pulled a bit of dried kumquat from the pocket of her dress and offered to share it with her sister. As the girls pulled at the sweetmeat to divide it equally, an old woman came up the path to the house.

"Good evening," said the old woman. "Are you Ah-bi and Ah-lee?"

"Yes," said Ah-bi, who was older.

"Your mother asked me to come and stay the night with you," said the woman settling down on the steps. "I am your old aunt, and I met your mother on the road as I was coming this way. She said for me to come and sleep with you to protect you from evil spirits and evil people until she returned."

Ah-lee, although she was younger, was responsible beyond her years.

"Our mother told us not to let anyone come in," she said, looking at the old woman carefully.

"Oh, but I am your relative. Do you see how much I look like your mother?" The two girls looked at the old woman, and indeed, she did look like their mother. (Witches can look any way they please). "Besides," she added, reaching inside her dress, "I have brought you some plums from your mother."

Ah-bi and Ah-lee were delighted with the fruit. By the time they had sucked the sweet flesh from the plum seeds, they had forgotten all about their mother's warning. They sat with their guest until the sun set over the rice paddy and the moon rose behind the house. When the moon fingers touched the ginger lilies, they rose to go to bed.

When the guest stood up she brushed against the *baqua* sign, making it drop to the ground where it rolled under a banana tree. Ah-bi and Ah-lee jumped up to run after it, but the old aunt grabbed them in her strong fingers and stopped them.

"No, no," she said. "Wait until morning. You might be bitten by a snake if you go chasing after that sign at night. It's only a painted picture of an eye."

"But our *baqua* keeps evil spirits out of the house," explained Ah-lee.

"Never mind," said the old woman, stepping over the threshold. "I'm here to look after you so you won't need the *baqua* tonight."

From time to time the old aunt gnawed on something she pulled from her pocket. Soon they all got into bed with the old woman in the middle.

"What are you eating, Aunt?" asked Ah-lee as she snuggled down beside her relative who continued to make loud crunching noises.

"Peanuts," said the old lady. "Oh, how I love peanuts!" She chuckled to herself as she pinched Ah-be with one hand and Ah-lee with the other.

"May I have one?" asked Ah-lee. "I love peanuts, too."

But the old lady only pulled Ah-lee closer to her with one arm. She continued to pinch Ah-bi, who was taller and thinner, with her other hand.

"Peanuts, peanuts," she chuckled in such a harsh, cracked voice that chills like the winter wind slid down Ah-lee's spine. She tried to pull away but the old woman only held her tighter, chuckling, "Peanuts, peanuts."

Peanuts? Ah-lee suddenly remembered the whispered tales she had heard about the Tiger Witch who crunched the finger bones of the little children she caught *like peanuts*.

From the other side of the old woman, Ah-lee could hear the even, sleep-sodden breathing of Ah-bi. Ah-bi could always fall asleep faster than anyone.

"Ah-bi," whispered Ah-lee, but the old woman put her bony fingers across Ah-lee's mouth, and the little girl lay there with only her quick wits for company. There was no doubt in her mind now that their bedfellow was the wicked old Tiger Witch. She must run for help before it was too late, but the old witch held her close. She must think fast.

Presently, Ah-lee began to turn and twist and pitch about in the bed. "Ohhh," she moaned, "I need to go outside, Aunt."

"No," said the witch, "you must stay here."

"If I don't got outside you'll be sorry," warned Ah-lee.

"No," said the witch again, munching on a seemingly endless supply of crunchy fingers.

"Please," squealed Ah-lee. "Oh, you'll be sorry."

"I won't let you go," she said in her scratchy witch voice. "I promised your dear mother to take care of you. A snake or a scorpion might bite you when you go outside."

"But I must go. I have to, I have to," cried Ah-lee, raising her voice in hopes of waking Ah-bi. But Ah-bi slept peacefully. "Why not tie a string to my ankle, Aunt? Then you can hold the string and pull it to see if I'm safe. I have to go. The plums upset me."

"All right," grumbled the witch. "Hand me the string."

The old witch tied the long string to Ah-lee's ankle, and Ah-lee hobbled through the door into the yard. Ah-bi was still sleeping soundly.

Once outside, Ah-lee slipped the string from her foot and tied it to a tree. Oh, she must hurry, hurry, before Ah-bi became a pocketful of crunchy bones.

"I'm all right, Aunt," Ah-lee called. "You can feel the string, can't you?" She could see the string jerk. "Don't worry about me. I'll pull the string when I'm ready to come back to the house."

Ah-lee looked at the moonlit path that led through the rice paddy to the temple. Never had she left her own yard at night, but this was no time for fear. She plunged through the field as fast as her feet would take her. She knew the old priest could drive the witch from the house, and she beat on the temple door as brazenly as a grown person.

"Old priest!" she cried. "Come quickly. The Tiger Witch is at our house, and Ah-bi is in bed with her!"

The old Taoist priest lit a lamp and came sleepily to the door.

"Hold the light," he said. "I must find my horn and my gong. I can't kill witches with them, but I can drive them away."

Ah-lee lit the path as they hurried across the field. At the edge of Ah-lee's yard, they could hear the old witch calling in her rasping voice.

"Just a minute, Aunt. I'm coming. I only want to stop by the well and get a drink of water," answered Ah-lee.

"When you get into your house, fill a dish with egg, pork, rice and bean curd and set it on your doorstep," whispered the old priest. "I will slip inside the house. When I begin to blow my horn and beat my gong, fling open the door. The old witch will go outside to taste the food because she is a witch. Then shut the door very fast."

"I understand," whispered Ah-lee. "I'm coming, Aunt," she called. She knocked on the door and the old witch let her in.

"Get back in bed now," ordered the witch.

"I'm very hungry. First I must get myself some food," said Ah-lee, fumbling around the stove. She grabbed up some egg and bean curd with some pork and rice and ran to the door.

"What are you doing?" grumbled the witch. "Come back here. You can't go outside again."

"I only want a moonbeam of light so I can see if my rice and bean curd have bugs in them," hedged Ah-lee, pushing the dish onto the doorstep. From the corner of her eye, she could see the old priest slipping into the house.

Ah-lee flung the door wide at the precise moment that the old priest began to beat his sacred gong and blow his sacred horn with a noise so loud that Ah-bi woke up with a scream and the old witch, attracted by the food, ran out of the house.

Ah-lee slammed the door shut and the old witch was gone.

The priest made sure that the girls were settled back in bed and returned to his temple.

Just as Ah-bi and Ah-lee were falling asleep, they heard a great knocking at the door.

"Open up, it's Mother," cried the voice at the door. It was undoubtedly Mother's voice. (Witches can take any kind of voice they please.)

Ah-bi flung open the door, and to her horror the old witch rushed into the room again. "Ah, ha," cried the witch, "you forgot to put your *baqua* back on the door!"

Ah-bi gave a shriek and ran behind the stove while Ah-lee and the witch played a fierce game of chase around the room. Ah-lee finally got through the door and up to the top of the banyan tree.

"Come down," yelled the witch.

"All right," said Ah-lee sweetly. "I'll come down after I rest a minute. I know you are planning to eat us, but first I think I should tell you that I am very dirty from running in the muddy rice paddy. If you will bring me a kettle of boiling peanut oil I will clean myself with it and jump right into your mouth. I will taste much better that way.

The witch grumbled, but she agreed.

"Ah-bi, make a pot of very hot oil," called Ah-lee. "I'm going to fry somebody."

"I understand, sister," called Ah-bi. "I'll put it on to boil."

The old Tiger Witch stood under the banyan tree looking up at Ah-lee. "I'm not going to wait any longer. I'm coming to get you. You're too slow," she complained.

"Boil it faster. Blow up the fire, Ah-bi," called Ah-lee.

"I'm blowing, sister," called Ah-bi, huffing and puffing at the charcoal.

"I'm coming up," snapped the old witch.

"Wait one minute," cried Ah-bi. "Here I come with the oil. I'll take it right up the tree to Ah-lee, and I'll wash in it, too, while you eat Ah-lee."

Ah-bi climbed the banyan tree with the pot of boiling oil. The girls made believe that they were washing in the oil while the old witch paced below.

"Open your mouth, Aunt," called the girls. "Stand right below us and open your mouth."

"I'm getting ready to jump," cried Ah-lee.

The greedy old witch stood right below Ah-lee and opened her ugly mouth. Ah-lee and Ah-bi tipped the kettle of smoking hot oil so that it fell directly into the witch's mouth. With a tiger's roar, she fell writhing to the ground.

The girls watched as her body wilted into a stack of wet banyan leaves. At the same time, a ghostly tiger rose from the leaves and ran snarling into the bamboo thicket on the hill.

At last they knew that the old Tiger Witch was dead, but nevertheless they looked under the banana tree until they found the *baqua* eye which they hung back on the door post, in case any other witches were prowling.

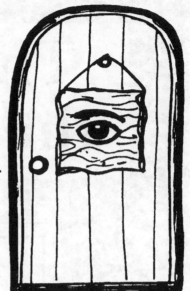

The next day their mother came back with the baby brother on her back, and one day later Father returned from his trip with the magistrate.

Everyone was so happy that they had a huge *pai-pai* feast. They had a parade and burned paper money to the gods and everyone ate all he could hold.

And no one ever saw the Tiger Witch again.

The Girl and the Tiger-Man

"*T*he Girl and the Tiger-Man" comes from the mountains of far eastern India, from a state called Manipur, but it may remind you of the European tale "Beauty and the Beast." The tiger-man who falls in love with the girl he kidnaps is known as Kabui-Keioiba. Unlike most victims in "knock at the door" tales, Thabat, the kidnapped girl, is able to save herself without any help.

There once lived a man who could become any shape he wanted to be. During the day he was usually a man, but at night he was a tiger that loved to prowl.

One day as he was searching for food the Tiger-man saw an old woman walking in the woods. "At last!" he said as he jumped in her path. "I'm starving."

"Wait!" said the woman in hopes of saving her life. "I'm as tough as I am old. I won't taste good. If you want sweeter flesh I can tell you where to find it."

The greedy Tiger-man agreed.

"There's a girl," said the woman. "Her name is Thabat. She's the only daughter in her family. Her seven brothers have left her alone while they work to earn her dowry."

As the old woman led the Tiger-man to the house where the girl was kept she told him what he had to do.

"She won't open the door to anyone except her brothers who always say a secret word. I know because I heard them say it one day and then go in the house."

The Tiger-man called out the word just like he'd been told to do, but Thabat yelled, "Go away." She knew the voice was far too rough to be one of her brothers.

This made the Tiger-man very angry because he still hadn't gotten anything to eat. He ran back to the old woman's house and said he'd settle for eating her after all.

"Just wait!" she told him. "You mustn't give up. I'll help. I'll make certain she opens the door."

This time the old woman called out the secret word in a voice that matched the brothers. It worked. Thabat joyfully opened the door, but was shocked to see the Tiger-man. Before she could scream he lept inside and carried her off. He'd intended to eat her for dinner, but Thabat was the most beautiful woman he'd ever seen. The more he ran the less he thought about eating her and the more he thought of marriage. The only thing Thabat could do to save herself was toss off clothes as they went along, leaving a trail for her brothers to find.

The Tiger-man did keep Thabat alive and in time she gave birth to a child. Though grateful to be alive, Thabat hated living in the Tiger-man's house. Every day she looked for a way to escape.

One day Thabat tried a new plan. She lied. She told the Tiger-man she loved him so much she wanted to stay with him for the rest of her life. The Tiger-man was so eager to have her love him he believed every word she said. Thinking Thabat loved him, he began to answer questions about his secret life. He even told her how he could change his shape at night and about the one thing that could kill him.

"But don't be afraid," he told her. "No one knows but you and me."

Not long after that Thabat asked the Tiger-man to go the river and fill a bamboo tube with water. It was part of her trick. The tube was hollow all the way through and couldn't hold anything. While the Tiger-man tried to fill the tube Thabat destroyed everything she could find in his house. She hated him so much for stealing her away she set his house on fire and left his child inside to die.

The Tiger-man was so blinded by love he didn't think for a moment that Thabat might be playing a trick. He felt so bad for not being able to fill up the bamboo tube he started home to apologize. When he got near enough to see his house in flames Thabat ran up and killed him with the secret he'd shared with her.

As Thabat traveled home, glad to be free, she met her brothers coming down the trail of clothes she'd left. All eight were very happy at being together again.

The Girl and the Tiger-Man

The Goat, the Kids, and the Bogey

*I*n this tale from the Embu people of Kenya in eastern Africa the villain is a Bogey— a cannibalistic, nonhuman creature with magical powers. Like Thabat in "The Girl and the Tiger-Man," these kids find a way to save themselves. When the children have their heads shaved, it is part of a traditional ceremony for purification and growing up. A unique twist at the end of this version echoes the knock at the door at the beginning of the story.

A goat once went to a pit and produced a family, but a Bogey saw her. And she had four children: the first was named "Kathengi Matumu"; the second was "Mathangu"; the third was "Kakomonge," and the fourth was "Mwenda Kuongo." And the goat called her children to give them milk, and she said: "Beware, there is a Bogey behind the house." Then she went out, and the Bogey came and called the kids in a deep voice. But they knew that the voice was not their mother's, and they only jeered at the Bogey. And this happened three times.

So the Bogey went to a wizard for assistance, and the wizard said: "You must go to the *siafu* (biting ant) to get your tongue shaved down, and then your voice will sound like the mother goat's." So the Bogey did this, though the ants hurt most terribly, and it was only possible to get a small piece of the tongue cut down each day. But at last the tongue was small enough, and the Bogey went and called to the children of the goat. So the kids all came out, and the Bogey ate three of them, but the eldest, "Kathengi Matumu," asked to be spared, saying that he would be a slave to the Bogey if he were spared. So she spared him, and took him home to her house. Soon after this the Bogey had a child, and when the child was big enough it went with Kathengi Matumu to watch the crops, to prevent all the wild animals from eating them. Then one day Kathengi Matumu took a spear and sharpened it, and stabbed a baobab-tree, and said: "When this tree dies the eater of my brothers will die." But the child of the Bogey grew angry, and threatened to tell its mother. But Kathengi Matumu said: "I was only in fun." However, the next day the same thing took place, and this time the Bogey's child told its mother. But the mother asked Kathengi Matumu, and he said: "It was only a charm to kill all the animals that come to eat the crops." But the next day the tree fell down, and Kathengi Matumu killed the Bogey's child, and skinned it. He took the meat to the Bogey, and said: "This is the meat of one of the animals that eat your crops, and your child has stopped behind to watch the skin, which is put out to dry." Then Kathengi Matumu sharpened a spear; and the Bogey said: "Where is my child?" And he said: "Only just behind." But the Bogey asked again, so Kathengi Matumu said: "How can you ask, when you know that you ate it!" But the Bogey was very angry when the truth was told, and said to Kathengi Matumu: "I shall kill you as soon as I have sharpened my razor." But when the razor was sharp, Kathengi Matumu did not wait to be attacked, but stabbed the Bogey with his spear." But he heard a voice inside from his eldest brother, which said, "Don't kill me," and the brother came out. Then Kathengi Matumu stabbed again, and his second brother was recovered in the same way, and the Bogey died. Then they all went home to their mother, who had remained living in the same place all the time. They called at the door, but their mother refused to believe them at first, saying: "How can you be my children, even if you have their voices, since my children were all eaten by the Bogey?" But at last she believed them, and they went into the house, and they all lived happily together after that, having been shaved on their return home.

The Goat, the Kids, and the Bogey

Tale Notes

Notes

The brief notes for each tale that follow cite the published sources used in preparing this collection and give information on related versions of each story. They also honor the lives of those who loved the tales and passed them on. The people and cultures that share these tales have often struggled like the seven little kids to survive the temporary threat and domination of a consuming wolf-like outsider. References here to history's flow of people, power, and events are not made to claim a tale's geneology but to establish the strength of the tale's spirit and the persistence of peoples' need to tell the story.

Although a great deal of written history in our schools is based on European awareness of the world, it is important that we do not confine a culture's sense of self, time, and value to Europe's view of history. Vanuatu, for example, was not "discovered" by outsiders. The indigenous people knew their world existed. And, it would have continued to exist if outsiders had never visited, let alone taken control. A secondary goal of these notes is to foster an awareness of the limitations of Eurocentric perspectives, both in the tale-related information we share with students *and* in the way we introduce the tales themselves.

When available, information about the teller as well as the date and place a tale was collected are included. Art, social, and geographical references are shared to help the reader/teller begin visualizing the tale in its home setting.

The Kid and the Wolf (Aesop, Greece)

Retold from *Aesop without Morals: The Famous Fables and a Life of Aesop* by Lloyd W. Daly (New York: Thomas Yoseloff, 1961) and *Babrius and Phaedrus* edited and translated by Ben Edwin Perry (Cambridge, MA: Harvard University Press, 1965).

Aesop, who lived in an area of Greece called Thrace during the sixth century B.C., created many stories in the oral tradition. Though he never published his stories, Aesop was well known. The early Greek writers Herodotus and Plutarch referred to him in their books. Demetrius published the first collection of Aesop's fables in the third century B.C., and Phaedrus later translated them from Greek into Latin verse in the middle of the first century A.D.

In classical times literature had to be verse if it was to be viewed as literature. Prose was for history and science. Aesop's fables continued to be retold throughout the Middle Ages and were among the first stories printed on presses. Both Rabbi Berechiach ha-Nakdan and Marie de France used Aesop's fables as sources for their fables in the twelfth century. Jean de la Fontaine created his famous poetic retellings in French during the last part of the seventeenth century.

Though Aesop's fable has remained essentially the same, some versions end with morals and some do not. There are also different points of view expressed in the morals. Phaedrus's retelling has no moral. Roger L'Estrange's moral states: "There was never any hypocrite so disguis'd, but he had some mark or other yet to be known by" (L'Estrange, 1931, 104). Daly's translation ends with the moral: "That it is laudable to obey the instruction of parents" (Daly, 1961, 306). The moral in Munro Leaf's 1941 retelling for children is clear and direct: "The Point—Mother knows best" (Leaf, 1941, 130).

Another Aesop fable, "The Wolf in Sheep's Clothing," shares this fable's theme of deceptive appearances.

Editions of Aesop's fables include:

Clark, Margaret. *The Best of Aesop's Fables.* Illustrated by Charlotte Voake (Boston: Joy Street Books, 1990).

Leaf, Munro. *Aesop's Fables.* Illustrated by Robert Lawson (New York: Heritage Reprints, 1941).

L'Estrange, Roger. *Fables of Aesop.* Illustrated by Alexander Calder (New York: Dover, [1931] 1967).

McKendry, John J. *Aesop: Five Centuries of Illustrated Fables* (New York: Metropolitan Museum of Art, 1964).

Rice, Eve. *Once in a Wood: Ten Tales from Aesop* (New York: Greenwillow, 1979).

Untermeyer, Louis. *Aesop's Fables.* Illustrated by Alice and Martin Provensen (New York: Golden Press, 1966).

The Wolf and the Kids (La Fontaine, France)

Reprinted from *The Fables of La Fontaine.* Translated by Margaret Wise Brown (New York: Harper, 1940).

Jean de la Fontaine wrote his interpretations of this and many other fables by Aesop between 1668 and 1694. He wrote with such clever rhymes that most people believe his fables can never be adequately translated into English verse. This prose translation was done by Margaret Wise Brown, who is best known for her picture book *Goodnight Moon.* The quality of La Fontaine's retellings made the fables a staple in France, and children there continue to know his fables well.

Other translation of La Fontaine include:

Marsh, Edward. *La Fontaine's Fables.* Illustrated by Alexander Calder (London: Dent & Sons, 1952).

Moore, Marianne. *The Fables of La Fontaine* (New York: Viking, 1964).

Four Disobedient Kids (Czecho-Slovak: Czechoslovakia)

Retold from *The Disobedient Kids and Other Czecho-Slovak Fairy Tales* by Bozena Nemcova. Interpreted by William H. Tomas and V. Smetanka. Selected by Dr. V. Tille (Prague: Koci, 1921).

Bozena Nemcova wrote and published her retellings of this and other Czecho-Slovak folktales around 1850 while living in the area of Europe known as Southern Bohemia. Nemcova viewed the stories as part of a growing effort to revive the local culture and folklore that had been repressed for many years by German rule. The authorities viewed her folktales as a defiant act and forced her husband to change jobs. In 1855 Nemcova published *The Grandmother,* one of the most widely read works of Czech literature. The English edition of her tales was published nearly 70 years later in 1921 after the country called Czechoslovakia had been formed following World War I.

The Goat and the Kids (Mordvin: Russia)

Reprinted from *Siberian and Other Folk Tales: Primitive Literature of the Empire of the Tsar* collected and translated by Charles Fillingham Coxwell (London: C.W. Daniel, 1925). Coxwell's source was the Russian-language edition *Collection of Mordvinian Ethnology* by A.A. Shakhmatov (1910).

The Mordvins are a minority race who settled long ago in the eastern part of the country of Russia along the Volga River. They are more closely related to the Finns than the Russians. Centuries ago they often overpowered the Russians. When this tale was collected the Mordvins were best known for the quality of their farming, beekeeping, and woodcarving. Since 1900 the Mordvins have been assimilating into the culture of Russia. In 1960 they ceased being an automous republic and became part of the Russian Republic in the coalition of countries then known as the Union of Soviet Socialist Republics (now known as the Commonwealth of Independent States).

Russian variants from the same geographic area include "The Wolf and the Goat," also in this collection. Finnish and Lappish language variants can be traced through *The Types of the Folktale: A Classification and Bibliography,* 2d rev. ed., by Stith Thompson (Helsinki: Folk Lore Fellows Communications Number 184, 1961).

The Devil Hammers His Tongue (Grenada)

Reprinted from *Folk-Lore of the Antilles, English and French* by Elsie Clews Parsons (Memoirs of the American Folk-Lore Society. Volume 26 Part 1) (New York: American Folk-Lore Society, 1933).

Parsons collected this tale from Edward Dowe, a 13-year-old schoolboy living in St. George, Grenada, of the Lesser Antilles in the Caribbean Sea.

It is said that Columbus saw the islands from a distance in 1498 and named them Concepcion. The original Carib peoples of Grenada were largely killed off by the French. The French and English fought over the island, often called Isle of Spice, until the English took control in 1783. As in most parts of the West Indies, the language, lore, and customs are a blend of all the people who moved to the area whether by choice or force. Today the people of Grenada are a blend of black Africans, multi-racial, East Indians, Anglos, and a small percentage of Caribs. Grenada gained its independence in 1974, and English remains the dominant language.

Related Variants

"Abused Child: Devil Files His Tongue" in *Suriname Folk-Lore* by Melville J. Herskovits and Frances S. Herskovits (New York: AMS Press, [1936] 1969).

In this variant the mother has four children named Minimini, Fremanboni, Fremantaria, and Koprokanu. The tale closes with the statement, "That shows that when you have many children you must love them all alike." Music is included for the mother's song. In his notes Herskovits refers to an unpublished variant he collected in Dahomey on the west coast of Africa.

"One, My Darling, Come to Mama" in *The Magic Orange Tree and Other Haitian Tales* collected by Diane Wolkstein (New York: Knopf, 1978).

In this variant there are four daughters, but only the fourth and unloved one has a name, Philamandre. When the mother returns and finds her three favorite daughters gone, she goes crazy with grief and abandons the fourth daughter to wander aimlessly singing her song. Philamandre goes off on her own, finds work, and eventually marries a prince. Years later after she has become queen a mad woman shows up singing the song meant to open the door. Philamandre recognizes her mother and takes her in saying, "The others are no more. But I am here. . . . You did not care for me, but I am here, and now I will take care of you." Music for the song is included.

The Story of the Wolf and the Goat (Kermani: Iran)

Reprinted from *Persian Tales* translated by D.C.R. Lorimer (London: Macmillan, 1919).

This tale was collected in the Kermani or southeastern section of Persia early in the twentieth century. The word Kerman also refers to a particular kind of Persian rug that was made in the area featuring muted colors and elaborate border patterns. Since 1935 Persia has been known as Iran. The history of the Persians and their land, which is two-thirds desert, stretches back to the ancient ruins of Persepolis built over 2500 years ago. Persian culture has been influenced by Greece, then later Arab and Mongol cultures as each came to dominate the area. At one time Persia grew to include Turkey, Iraq, Palestine, Pakistan, and beyond. Later, as boundaries and power shifted again, Persia became part of the Turkish Ottoman Empire. It has been an Islamic culture since the seventh century. Raising sheep and goats is the primary source of income for many rural Iranians.

Related Variants

"The Ewe, the Goat and the Lion" (Kurdistani-Jew), in this collection, shares the same final scene. The mother battles the newly toothless villain and saves her children by goring the villain with her horns.

"The Goat and the Wolf" in *Four Tales from Asia for Children Everywhere* (Book Six) by the Asian Cultural Center for Unesco. (New York: Weatherhill, 1977).

This variant from Afghanistan shares the same concluding action, but focuses on the mother's role. The three kids' experience with a knock at the door is distilled to a single sentence.

The Wolf and the Goat (Russia)

Reprinted from *Russian Fairy Tales* collected by Aleksandr Afanas'ev. Translated by Norbert Guterman (New York: Pantheon, 1945).

Afanas'ev was a lawyer by education and began publishing Russian folktales in 1866. He only recorded a few of the tales himself. The rest in his collection were borrowed from earlier works by the Russian Geographical Society and Vladimir Dahl. It was rare that any of the collectors noted the source or place when a tale was recorded. The governments of Russia have changed greatly since 1866, but this tale remains a popular one. It was included in a 1975 edition published in English by the Soviet Union, *The Little Clay Hut*.

Russia is the name of a race or ethnic group of people *and* the name of a geographic area that includes many ethnic groups in addition to Russians. Originally Slavs from eastern Europe, the Russians adopted Eastern Orthodoxy as their religion around the year 1000. Descendents of the Mongol ruler Ghengis Khan over took Russia in the early thirteenth century, and their dominance lasted nearly 150 years. Tsar Peter the Great pushed for Russians to accept the western ways of Europe during the eighteenth century. Russia experienced a major revolution in 1917 and became part of the newly created Union of Soviet Socialist Republics. When the U.S.S.R. dismantled itself in 1991 because of public demand, the Russian people played a vital role.

Related Variants

Adolph Gerber cites two variants in his *Great Russian Animal Tales* (Franklin, [1891] 1970). The first, which comes from the government of Saratov, is very close to the one reprinted here. The second contains several different elements. The wolf tricks the kids and devours all but one, leaving only their hair and bones. As revenge the mother goat grinds the hair and bones into a pastry and invites both fox and wolf for breakfast. After they eat the goat convinces them to join her in her favorite game of jumping over a hole in the floor. The goat and fox succeed. The wolf falls into the cellar and is burned to death on hot coals and iron rods. The survivors feast, and the goat lives happily with her remaining child.

"The Kids and the Wolf" in *Still More Russian Picture Tales* by Valery Carrick (New York: Dover, [1915] 1970) p. 15-22.

This variant is similar to "The Goat and the Kids" (Mordvin) in this collection. The tale ends with all the kids being devoured.

"The Wolf and the Seven Little Kids" in *The Little Clay Hut: Russian Folk Tales about Animals* translated by Irina Zheleznova et al. Drawings by Evgeny Rachev (USSR: Progress Publishers 1975) p. 24-31.

This variant is similar to "The Wolf and the Goat" collected by Afanas'ev.

"The Goat and Her Three Kids" in *Folk Tales from Roumania* translated from the *Roumanian of Ion Creagna* by Mable Nandris (New York: Roy, 1953).

This variant shares a fiery conclusion with the Russian variants and contains some unique elements as well. In the beginning the wolf is introduced to the audience as the kids' godfather who has sworn to never frighten them. Later, when the sole surviving kid asks if things shouldn't be left to the judgment of God, the mother goat says, "Oh no, my dear! For you must defend yourself." Her defense is to invite the wolf to a funeral feast. When he arrives she tricks him into sitting in a wax chair that eventually engulfs him in flames. As he burns the mother tosses more hay on the fire and pummels him with stones. The neighbors watch the wolf's demise without shedding a tear. Some are even pleased to see him die.

"The Fire Test" in *Nights with Uncle Remus* in *The Complete Tales of Uncle Remus* collected by Joel Chandler Harris (Boston: Houghton Mifflin, [1883] 1955) p. 297-302.

The cast of characters features rabbits rather than goats, but this African-American variant shares the trick of getting the villain to leap over a blazing fire. In this tale none of the children is recovered, and no one sheds a tear over the death of the wolf. Julius Lester includes a more accessible retelling in his collection *More Tales of Uncle Remus: Further Adventures of Brer Rabbit, His Friends, Enemies and Others* (Dial, 1988).

The Wolf and the Seven Little Kids (Germany)

Reprinted from *The Complete Grimms' Fairy Tales*. Translated by Margaret Hunt (New York: Pantheon, 1944).

This variant, first published by the Brothers Grimm, has become the best-known version of the tale in the United States. Jacob and Wilhelm Grimm were interested in tales for their literary and historical value. Their collection was part of their effort to restore and honor German literature as Germany struggled to become a unified nation rather than a handful of separate kingdoms.

The Grimms' tales were first published in English in the 1820s with translations by Edward Taylor and illustrations by George Cruikshank. Since then there have been translations around the world, and a never-ending list of illustrators have shared their interpretations of the tales. For some reason several editions of the tales in English changed the cast of characters to a fox or wolf tricking seven little geese. One of the first to do so, if not the first, was Lucy Crane in her 1882 translation, *Household Stories*, which was illustrated by her brother Walter Crane. Later editions of *Household Stories* reverted to featuring seven little kids.

Translated around the world, the Grimms' tales have surely had a broad influence on the stories children share. Several variants in this collection may well have been stimulated by the Grimms' collection, including "Los Seis Cabritos" (Mexico) and "The Goat and the Kids and the Bogey" (Embu: Kenya). A variant from Aiken, South Carolina, titled "The Five Kids" was collected by Elsie Clews Parson and published in *The Journal of American Folklore* 34 (1921):18.

Other translations of the Grimms include:

Bell, Anthea and Rogers, Anne. *The Best of Grimms' Fairy Tales* (New York: Larousse, 1979).

Crane, Lucy. *Household Stories* (New York: Dover, [1886] 1963).

Crossley-Holland, Kevin. *The Fox and the Cat: Animal Tales from Grimm* (New York: Lothrop, 1985).

Manheim, Ralph. *Grimms' Tales for Young and Old* (New York: Doubleday, 1977).

Shub, Elizabeth. *About Wise Men and Simpletons: Twelve Tales from Grimm* (New York: Macmillan, 1971).

Los Seis Cabritos (Mexico)

Reprinted from *Mexican Tales and Legends from Los Altos* by Stanley L. Robe (Berkeley: University of California Press, 1970).

Robe collected this tale in 1947 from a 26-year-old man named Pedro Gonzales in the small town of Acatic, Jalisco, in Mexico. Jalisco, is a state in west central Mexico that includes the famous city Guadalajara. At the time the tale was collected Acatic had no electricity or movie theater. Pedro Gonzales, a mechanic, had learned the tale from his mother, who told him stories when he was a child.

This area of Mexico has been influenced by Spanish culture since 1530; colonization began soon after that. The Catholic Church has also been very influential. As in much of Mexico, northern South America, and the Caribbean, there has been a long history of multicultural marriages and children.

This variant is interesting because it more closely resembles the German version of the tale than the Spanish one. Perhaps a Spanish translation of the Grimms' tales worked its way into oral tradition. Though this tale has not been published often in Mexico, Robe found it to be a well-known tale in the Los Altos area. Robe includes two other variants: "Los Siete Cabritos" and "La Chivita." The latter is unique in that the kids hide as a precaution as soon as their mother leaves, and the wolf appears carrying a basket of eggs.

Other Spanish-Language Variants

"La Vaca y el Becerrito" in *Spanish Folk-Tales from New Mexico* by Jose Manuel Espinosa (Memoirs of the American Folk-Lore Society, Vol. 30) (New York: American Folk-Lore Society, 1937) p. 186.

This variant features a cow who leaves her calf at home. Coyote is the devouring villain.

"Los Cabritos y el Lobo" in "Porto Rican Folk-Lore: Folk-Tales" by J. Alden Mason and edited by Aurelio M. Espinosa. *Journal of American Folklore* 40 (October-December, 1927): 348-50.

"Las Astucias del Zorro" in *El Folklore de los Niños* by Julio Aramburu (Buenos Aires: El Ateneo, 1944) p. 84-89.

This variant from Argentina features a fox who devours young rabbits.

A Granny Who Had Many Children (Yiddish: Canada)

Reprinted from *Folk Lore of Canada* collected by Edith Fowke (Toronto: McClelland and Stewart, 1976).

Canadian folk literature is a collage of domestic and imported stories. Native American and Inuit tales are Canada's original literature. Today Canadian folklore also includes tales brought by those who immigrated from other lands. Fowke's source for this tale was Ruth Rubin, who remembered it from her childhood in the Jewish community of Montreal. Jews were banned from Canada until Britain took control from France in the 1700s. Sizeable groups of Jews from Poland and Russia began to immigrate to Canada in the 1800s to escape persecution. Though a few moved to farms, most settled in Montreal and Toronto. In contrast to European/Christian-based versions of this tale, which feature animals, many Jewish versions feature a rabbi or family members like "A Granny Who Had Many Children."

Related Variants

"The Bear and the Children" in *The Diamond Tree: Jewish Tales from Around the World* selected and retold by Howard Schwartz and Barbara Rush. (New York: HarperCollins, 1991) p. 93-96.
This variant from Eastern Europe is one of the few to feature both mother and father. It is also unique because the mother fills the villain's stomach with bread instead of stones and lets him live.

"The Ewe, the Goat and the Lion" (Kurdistani-Jew) is included in this collection.

Noy, Dov. *The Jewish Animal Tale of Oral Tradition* (Haifa: Haifa Municipality, 1976).
This volume indexes several variants in other languages including Roumanian and Lithuanian. Some feature a rabbi and his wife who have either three or seven children.

"Wolf and Goats" in *Fables of a Jewish Aesop* translated from the *Fox Fables of Berechiah ha-Nakdan* by Moses Hadas (New York: Columbia University Press, 1964) p. 44-45

Yiddsche Folkmeisses (Vilna: Yiddish Scientific Institute) by Y.L. Cahan includes variants in both the 1931 and 1940 editions.

Tagaro's Fish (Vanuatu)

Retold from "How Tagaro the Little Found Fish" in *The Melanesians: Studies in Their Anthropology and Folk-Lore* by Robert H. Codrington (Oxford, Clarendon Press, 1891).

This variant was collected on Leper's Island in 1890. Codrington had his sources write their stories, which he then translated into English. Leper's Island is a small island in the archipelago known as New Hebrides. Today these islands, east of northern Australia, are called Vanuatu.

Tagaro and his enemy Mera-mbuto are important figures in Melanesian tales. According to legends, Tagaro descended from heaven, created things on earth, and returned to heaven. A knowing, powerful, and kind figure, he has no bodily form except on earth where he appears as a human. His name is often associated with sacred places. One legend says that Leper's Island was once Tagaro's canoe.

Melanesia was first noticed by Europeans in the sixteenth century. As with most Pacific islands, a variety of countries have claimed land and influenced local culture. Initially two-thirds of the indigenous Papuan population were killed by raiders and diseases they brought. Today the population is a blend of Papuans, Europeans, Chinese, and those from other Pacific islands. An English-Melanesian pidgin language is now the official language.

Related Variants

"Tio Manube" in *Mono-Alu Folklore (Bouganville Strait, Western Solomon Islands)* by Gerald Camden Wheeler (London: Routledge & Sons, 1926) p. 214-16.

This variant features two brothers, but only one fish. After tracking down the villain and killing him the brothers eat the fish.

The Cunning Snake (African-American: U.S)

Retold from "The Cunning Snake" in *Nights with Uncle Remus: Myths and Legends of the Old Plantation in The Complete Tales of Uncle Remus* by Joel Chandler Harris (Boston: Houghton, [1883] 1955).

Harris collected this tale and many others in the early 1880s from African-Americans who had lived as slaves before the Civil War. Harris usually had his fictional character Uncle Remus tell the tales, but in some cases, such as "The Cunning Snake," the fictional storyteller was Daddy Jack. Harris had a good ear for language and worked hard to capture the teller's rhythms and dialect. Some linguists and folklorists believe the dialect Harris recorded has strong ties to the Hausa people in Nigeria. Others believe the tales are more closely related to the Ashanti and Yoruba people of northwest Africa.

Harris' books of African-American folktales are some of the best-known collections of tales in U.S. history. They have also been some of the most controversial. The fictional device of a happy slave telling the tales to white children has troubled many people. Especially troubling is the depiction of Uncle Remus as a man "who had nothing but pleasant memories of the discipline of slavery." The folktales without the artifice of Uncle Remus continue to be very popular. Margaret Wise Brown, Julius Lester, and Van Dyke Parks have all published new editions of these tales in language more accessible to contemporary readers.

Related Variants

Nights with Uncle Remus contains three other tales that are in some way related to "The Wolf and the Seven Little Kids." "Cutta Cord La" is discussed in the notes following "When a Wise Man Dies." "The Fires Test" is discussed in the notes following "The Wolf and the Goat." Harris' vari-

ant of "The Three Little Pigs" also contains a knock at the door and a deceitful voice. Called "The Story of The Pigs," this tale has wolf tricking the first three pigs into opening their doors by saying he is a friend of their late mother's. Wolf tries to trick the fifth or last pig by pretending to be one of the sibling pigs he's already devoured. The littlest pig doesn't fall for the trick and burns the wolf when he tries to climb down the chimney. Julius Lester includes a retelling of this tale titled "Brer Wolf and the Pigs" in *Further Tales of Uncle Remus* (Dial, 1990).

"The Goat, the Kids and the Wolf" (France)

Reprinted from *Folktales from France* edited by Genevieve Massignon. Translated by Jacqueline Hyland (Chicago: University of Chicago Press, 1968).

This variant was recorded in 1959 from a 79-year-old peasant woman in Montjean. Versions of this tale can be traced in print back to 1886. In *Contes Populaires de Lorraine*, Emmanuel Cosquin refers to many French variants. Charles Coxwell cites several French variants including one with a unique plot twist in his notes for *Siberian and Other Folk Tales* (London: Daniel, 1910). After dipping his paw in lime the wolf succeeds in tricking the kids to open the door, but he is only able to devour two of them. Because of this the wolf repeats his trick two more times, devouring more kids on each visit. Paul Delarue reports he found 60 variants in *The Borzoi Book of French Folk Tales* which was compiled in the 1940s and 1950s. Genevieve Massignon also cites two variants that feature a sow and a hen instead of goats.

France began developing a central government in Paris in the tenth century. As Europe began exploring the rest of the globe France claimed many areas of the world as their colonies, including sections of Africa, Asia, Melanesia, and the Caribbean. Despite its strong central government, France remains today a country of major regional contrasts and languages.

Related Variants

"The Goat and Her Kids" in *The Borzoi Book of French Folk Tales* by Paul Delarue. Translated by Austin E. Fife (New York: Knopf, 1956) p. 300-03.

This variant begins with the mother breaking her leg and going to get it splinted. She has only three kids. When the wolf tricks his way into the house he is only able to eat one kid and the tail of the second. The third hides safely in a wooden shoe. When the mother returns she tricks the wolf into scalding himself and he vomits up the first kid and second kid's tail before running away.

"The Goat Who Lied" in *Folktales from France* edited by Genevieve Massignon. Translated by Jacqueline Hyland (Chicago: University of Chicago Press, 1968) p. 71-73.

This variant has a longer beginning that details how the mother goat lied and had her leg broken by her master as punishment. She is not able to rescue her one kid from the wolf, but she does scald him to death.

"The Mother Goat and Her Five Children" in *Picture Tales from the French* by Simone Chamoud (New York: Stokes, 1933) p. 105-10.

In this variant five little kids are threatened but never caught. Mother and kids then trick the wolf into coming down the chimney into the fire. After he is burned the wolf runs off looking "more like a sausage than a wolf."

Other French language variants can be found in:

Barbeau, C-Marius. "Contes Populaires Canadiens." *Journal of American Folklore* 29 (1916): 141-50.

Carriere, Joseph Medard. *Tales from the French Folk-Lore of Missouri* (Evanston, IL: Northwestern University, 1937) p. 23-24.

Cosquin, Emmanuel. *Contes Populaires de Lorraine* (Paris, 1886).

Parsons, Elsie Clews. *Folk-Lore of the Antilles, French and English* (Memoirs of the American Folk-Lore Society, Vol. 26) (New York: American Folk-Lore Society, 1933-44) I:216, III: 60, 500.

When a Wise Man Dies, a Wise Man Buries Him (Cameroon)

Reprinted from *Some Day Been Day: West African Pidgin Folktales* by Loreto Todd. (London: Routledge & Kegan Paul, 1979).

This variant was collected by Professor Todd in the Bamenda Grassfield in 1966 while she was living in Cameroon. Most of the tales were told in Pidgin in the evenings after supper. Todd translated them at a later date. Cameroon has long been a crossroads of cultures. Today this country located on the west coast of Africa includes 200 ethnic groups. Works of local art date back as far as the fifth century B.C. The area was first visited by Europeans in 1472 when the Portuguese explorer Fernao de Po passed by the coast. Slave traders began arriving in the early 1500s. Children and elders were often subject to famine like the one in "When a Wise Man Dies" when slave traders took all the adults who worked in the fields. By turn Germany, France, and Britain have all ruled over Cameroon. When France controlled the area, people who did not adopt European clothes, language, and manners were penalized. Today Cameroon is a free country with laws protecting all area religions including Christianity, Islam, and traditional African religions. The Pidgin language is a mixed language that developed out of a need for people of different nationalities and languages to communicate in trade. Though French and English are the official languages of Cameroon, Cameroon Pidgin is highly developed and the most commonly heard language.

Related Variants

Several differences appear in these variants. A treehouse or place in the clouds replaces the house, and a call to pull up the rope replaces the knock at the door. The roles of an adult protecting a hidden child are reversed in most of these variants, with the reason for hiding the parent being to save her from being eaten during a time of starvation. See Motif K231.1.1—Mutual agreement to sacrifice family and K944—Deceptive agreement to kill family.

"Antelope's Mother: The Woman in the Moon" in *Olde the Hunter and Other Tales from Nigeria* by Harold Courlander and Ezekiel A. Eshugbayi. (New York: Harcourt, 1968) p. 72-76.

In hopes of saving his mother from being eaten Antelope puts her on the moon and visits when she throws down a rope. Other animals try to get her to pull up the rope, but they fail. In this tale the rope is cut when the mother tries to protect herself from the hungry animals and ends up stranded on the moon.

"Cutta Cord-La" in *Afro-American Folktales: Stories from Black Traditions in the New World* selected and edited by Roger D. Abrahams (New York: Pantheon) p. 144-46. The same basic tale appears in *Nights with Uncle Remus* in *The Complete Tales of Uncle Remus* by Joel Chandler Harris. (Boston: Houghton, [1883] 1955) p. 289-92.

Brer Wolf and Brer Rabbit agree to kill their grandmothers for food, but Brer Rabbit hides his granny at the top of a coconut tree. Brer Wolf alters his voice to sound like Brer Rabbit and tricks granny into pulling up the rope. When Brer Rabbit sees what is happening he yells for his granny to cut the rope or "cutta cord-la." Wolf ends up crashing to the ground and breaking his neck.

"The Hyena and the Bitch" in "Fifty Hausa Folk-Tales" by A.J.N. Tremearne *Folklore* 21(1910): 492-93.

A mother dog puts her puppies in a tree for safety, but angry hyena learns the mother's chant and tricks the puppies into letting down the rope. Just before hyena reaches the top of the tree the puppies realize what is happening and drop hyena to the ground.

"Oh No, Not My Mother!" in *Tortoise the Trickster and Other Folktales From Cameroon* by Loreto Todd. (New York: Shocken, 1979) p. 48-52.

This is basically the same tale as reprinted in this collection but retold in more traditional English rather than Pidgin.

"Why the Baboon Has a Shining Seat" in *Singing Tales of Africa* retold by Adjai Robinson (New York: Scribners, 1974) p. 9-15.

This variant is from the Krio people of Sierra Leone. The cast features Bra Rabbit, his mother at the top of a tree, Bra Baboon, and other animals who try to get rabbit's hidden food. Music for the song is included.

"Why the Tortoise's Shell is Cracked and Crooked" in *Nigerian Folk Tales* as told by Olawale Idewa and Omotayo Adu. Edited by Barbara Walker. (New York: Rutgers, 1961) p. 27-29.

Turtle is the villain in this variant and easily alters his voice to fool dog into pulling up the rope. But once dog sees he's pulling up turtle he cuts the rope, and turtle crashes to the ground.

La Belle Venus (Haiti)

Reprinted from *How Donkeys Came to Haiti and Other Tales*. Retold by Gyneth Johnson (New York: Devin-Adair, 1949).

Johnson collected this tale in the early 1940s. She spent most of her time in CarreJour outside Port au Prince and attended many storytelling gatherings. Like the versions from Vanuatu, Korea, and Japan in this collection, "La Belle Venus" is a "pourquoi" tale, which explains how and why something in nature came to be.

Haiti is located on the western side of the Caribbean island of Hispaniola. After European explorers first claimed the island in the 1600s, many of the indigenous Carib people were shipped to Spain as slaves. Most Haitians today are descendents of West Africans brought over as slaves during the sixteenth and seventeenth centuries. In 1791 a group of rebel slaves seized control of the country. Though the uprising was squelched, Haitians eventually won their freedom from France in 1804. Haiti's history has remained one of racism and violence with a small number of wealthy elite and massive numbers of poor. U.S. troops ruled the country from 1915 to 1934. French is the official language, but the language spoken by most is a creole blend of French laced with Spanish and West African words. Most Haitians also practice a blend of Catholicism and voodoo.

"Father Found" is a tale from the Bahamas similar to "La Belle Venus." See notes for "Tiger Softens His Voice" (Jamaica).

Other "pourquoi" variants include:

"Antelope's Mother: The Woman in the Moon." See notes for "When a Wise Man Dies, a Wise Man Buries Him" (Cameroon).

"The Golden Chain from Heaven" (Japan) in this collection.

"The Sun and the Moon" (Korea) in this collection.

"Tagaro's Fish" (Melanesia) in this collection.

"Why the Baboon Has a Shining Seat." See notes for "When a Wise Man Dies, a Wise Man Buries Him" (Cameroon).

Tiger Softens His Voice (Jamaica)

Reprinted from *Jamaica Anansi Stories* by Martha Warren Beckwith. (Memoirs of the American Folk-Lore Society, Volume 17). (New York: American Folk-Lore Society, 1924).

Like many folktales, this variant has a multinational history. Martha Warren Beckwith collected tales in Jamaica in 1919 and 1921. This tale was told to her by George Parkes, who had heard it while visiting Cape Coast, Ghana.

Today 90 percent of the people in Jamaica have African ancestors, but when Columbus visited the island in 1494 it was populated by Arawak Indians who suffered greatly at the hands of the outsiders. The island belonged to the Columbus family during the 1500s and later became a British territory in 1655. British forces were continually attacked by freed slaves throughout the eighteenth century, and slavery was finally abolished in 1830. Today Jamaica is an independent country within the Commonwealth of Great Britain and known as the home of reggae music. English is the official language, but Jamaican English includes many African words.

"Father Found" in *Folktales of Andros Island, Bahamas* by Elsie Clews Parsons (Memoirs of the American Folk-Lore Society, Vol. 13) (New York: American Folk-Lore Society, 1918) p. 35-37.

This variant is told in dialect and is different in two key ways. A king's soldiers knock on the door and echo the song the young woman's father sang. Instead of being devoured by those who trick her into opening the door, she ends up marrying the prince. When her father later appears outside the castle singing, father and daughter are reunited. See also "One My Darling, Come to Mama" in notes for "The Devil Hammers His Tongue."

"La Belle Venus" in this collection.

"Leah and Tiger" in *Jamaican Song and Story* edited by Walter Jekyll (London: David Nutt, 1907) p. 108-12.

Told in dialect, this variant is virtually the same story as "Why Women Won't Listen" (see below) but without the blatantly sexist ending. Music is included for the song.

"Lion Makes His Voice Clear" in "Folk-Lore from Antigue, British West Indies" by John H. Johnson *Journal of American Folk-lore* 34(1921): 69-70.

"Tiger's Wife" in *Folk-Lore of the Sea Islands, South Carolina* by Elsie Clews Parsons (Memoirs of the American Folk-Lore Society, Vol. 16) (New York: American Folk-Lore Society, 1923) p. 50-51.

This variant is told in dialect. Primary characters are two tigers and rabbit who steals the tiger's wife.

"Why Women Won't Listen" in *West Indian Folk-Tales* retold by Philip Sherlock (London: Oxford University Press, 1964) p. 112-17.

This variant is unusual in that the daughter is put in a separate place away from home for safe keeping. After a while she asks to be taken back home, but her mother says not until her father gives his permission. By the time he gives his permission for her to leave the hiding place the tiger has tricked and killed her. The mother dies of grief and guilt. The father soon dies of grief as well.

The tale concludes with the reason that all this happened "because women are so obstinate. Their ears are hard, so they do not listen, and because they do not do what they are told, this kind of thing occurs."

The Jackal and the Lambs (Kabyl: Algeria)

Reprinted from *African Genesis* by Leo Frobenius and Douglas C. Cox (New York: Stackpole, 1937).

This variant was collected by Frobenius in the early 1920s and first published in German.

This Kabyls are one group in the larger ethnic group known as the Berbers of North Africa. Many Kabyls are centered in the isolated Djurdjura mountains east of Algers City, Algeria. There the woods resemble Europe's, with oak and ash trees. The Kabyls trace their history back to the eighth century when they were converted to Islam by the Arabs. Because of the mountainous landscape some people believe the Kabyls were not as influenced by Arab rule and remain closer to ancient Berber traditions. Rather than nomadic, the Kabyls are traditionally farmers and known for their olives, figs, and goats. They are also known for their homes, which they value highly. The jackal is a frequent villain in Berber tales and lamb is a popular dish. There are many Berber dialects and many people in North Africa speak Arabic as a second language.

Related Variants

"The Little She-Goat" (Palestinian-Arab) in this collection.

The Ewe, the Goat and the Lion (Kurdistani-Jew)

Reprinted from *The Folk Literature of the Kurdistani Jews: An Anthology* translated from Hebrew and Neo-Aramic by Yona Sabar (New Haven: Yale University Press, 1982).

Sabar's source for this tale was the Israel Folktale Archives, established in 1955. Abraham Nisan recorded the tale from his grandfather, who was a native of Iraqi Kurdistan.

For centuries the Kurdistani Jews lived in the rugged mountains of Kurdistan—an area overlapping eastern Turkey, northern Iraq, and northwestern Iran. The Kurds, a non-Arabic people, have long been dismissed as an ethnic group. There is even a Kurdish proverb that states: "The Kurds have no friends." Most Kurds are Sunni Muslim, while only a small percentage are Jews. The Kurdistani Jews trace their ancestry to the original exiles from the land of Israel in the first century. Isolated in the mountains, their folklore changed little over the years. More Jews migrated to Kurdistan during the persecution of the European crusades. Kurdistani Jews began returning to the land of Israel as early as 1812. Since Israel was declared a nation, almost all Kurdistani Jews have immigrated to Israel and begun to assimilate into contemporary Hebrew-Israeli culture.

Related Variants

"How the Fox Took a Turn Out of the Goat" in *Popular Tales of the West Highlands,* Volume III, by John F. Campbell (London: Gardner, 1892. Reprint, Detroit: Singing Tree Press, 1964) p. 103-05.

This Gaelic version is told by Hector Boyd of Barra. In his footnote Campbell summarizes a more interesting variant he collected in 1861 from Alexander Carmichael from Carbost in Skye. Upon finding her children missing the mother goat goes searching the houses of gull, hoodie (a type of crow), and sheep before stopping at fox's house. The fox invites her in, eats a big meal in front of her, and then orders her to scratch his stomach. The goat rips him open, freeing her kids, and takes them home.

"The Story of the Wolf and the Goat" (Persia) in this collection.

"The Goat and the Wolf" in *Four Tales from Asia for Children Everywhere* (Book Six) by the Asian Cultural Center for Unesco (New York: Weatherhill, 1977).

This variant from Afghanistan focuses on the mother's role in the story and distills the drama of the knock at the door to a single sentence.

The Water of Ladi (Hausa: Nigeria)

Reprinted from Hausa *Folk-Lore, Customs, Proverbs, Etc.* by R. Sutherland Rattray. Volume II (Oxford: Clarendon Press, 1913).

The Hausa language is written using Arabic characters, though some recent writing has been done in the Roman alphabet. Many older sources of Hausa folktales were written in the Arabic language. Rattray was greatly helped in compiling tales by a Malam or scribe who could translate Arabic into Hausa. The arts have long played a respected role in Hausa culture, and scribes are some of the most honored members of a Hausa community. Crafts have also been a vital element in the Hausa economy.

The Hausa people live primarily in the open savanna and desert areas of southwest Nigeria and southern Niger where water is greatly valued. They are believed to have once migrated from near Ethiopia, later mixing with Arabs, Berbers, Copts, and others between the Nile and Niger rivers. Islam came to the Hausa in the thirteenth century and was firmly established after a religious war in the 1800s. The Hausa have long had a sophisticated social system of classes that once ranged from aristocracy to peasants to slaves. For more background on the Hausa, please see notes for "Journey to the Mending City."

Related Variants

"Why Hawa Prevented the Beasts from Drinking" in *Fables and Fairy Tales for Little Folk or Uncle Remus in Hausaland* by Mary and A.J.N. Tremearne (Cambridge: Heffer & Sons, 1910) n.p.

"Journey to the Mending City" in this collection.

"The Hyena and the Bitch." See notes for "When A Wise Man Dies, a Wise Man Buries Him."

Carlanco (Spain)

Retold from *Picture Tales from Spain* by Ruth Sawyer (New York: Stokes, 1936) and *Spanish Fairy Tales* by Fernan Cabellero (Philadelphia: Lippincott, n.d.)

In Spain the basic story of the wolf knocking at the little goat's door can be traced in fable form back to 1489 with the publication of *Ysopete Ystoriado*. The longer, folktale version included here is unusual when compared to most European versions. Like many Asian and African versions, it has a fantasy villain, Carlanco, rather than a natural animal of prey.

Over the years the land and people of Spain have been influenced by many overpowering cultures and later influenced many other cultures in their efforts to colonize the world. Greek traders left their mark on early Spain, then the Celts of western Europe. Carthaginians from northern Africa also came to Spain before one A.D. The Romans later gave them Latin and Christianity. Catholicism became the official religion, but in less than 100 years Muslims from North Africa had taken over Spain, and Islam became the dominant religion for nearly 800 years. Elegant, ornate examples of Islamic architecture remain among Spain's art treasurers. Jews also contributed greatly to Spanish culture until they were expelled in 1492. Since the end of Islamic rule at the end of the fifteenth century Catholicism has remained a strong force in Spanish folklore. The wasp, for example, who helps the mother goat in "Carlanco" is called the Abbess, which is the female in charge of a convent of nuns.

The Rabbit and the Bear (Pennsylvania Dutch: U.S.)

Retold from "Pennsylvania German Folk Tales, Legends, Once-Upon-a-Time Stories, Maxims and Sayings" collected, translated, and edited by Thomas R. Brendle and William S. Troxell in *Pennsylvania German Society: Proceedings and Addresses at Fiftieth Anniversary* (Lancaster, PA. October 17,

1941) (Norristown, PA: Pennsylvania German Society, 1944).

Brendle and Troxell's source for this variant was Mrs. Emma Diehl of Freeberg, Pennsylvania, who told the tale in the German dialect known as Pennsylvania Dutch.

The term Pennsylvania Dutch is technically incorrect. The people known as Pennsylvania Dutch are of German ancestry, not Dutch. Although many Germans have immigrated to the United States, the Pennsylvania Dutch are those who moved to southeast Pennsylvania before a unified spirit of German nationality began to develop in the early 1800s. Some Pennsylvania Dutch houses date back before the Declaration of Independence, at a time when most colonists were British. The Amish and Mennonites are all descendents of the early Pennsylvania Dutch, but only a small percentage of the Pennsylvania Dutch are or were Amish and Mennonite.

Emigrating when they did and staying to themselves, their culture remained steeped in seventeenth- and eighteenth-century German tradition. This *could* mean that the core story of "The Rabbit and the Bear" came to the United States before the Grimms collected their German variant, "The Wolf and the Seven Little Kids."

The Story of Demane and Demazana (Xhosa: South Africa)

Reprinted from *Kaffir Folk-Lore: A Selection from the Traditional Tales Current among the People Living on the Eastern Border of the Cape Colony* by George McCall Theal (London: Sonnenschein, 1886. Reprint. Westport, CT: Negro Universities Press, 1970).

Theal heard this tale from several tellers in the 1860s and 1870s and then wrote his own composite retelling. Though he called his collection *Kaffir Folk-Lore* the word kaffir is no longer used in South Africa except by those who use it as a harsh, derogatory term. In his preface Theal states that his tales came from the Amoxosa people now identified as Xhosa. The Xhosa are descendants of the Ngoni people who migrated south from the

Limpopo River around 1300. They had developed metal smithing long before the first Europeans visited their area in 1688. Primarily farmers, the Xhosa battled with white settlers for over 100 years before being defeated. Today the Xhosa people are concentrated in the Transkei and Ciskei sections of the Cape Province area of South Africa. Bishop Desmond Tutu and Nelson Mandela were born in this area and spoke Xhosa as children.

Related Variants

"A Girl Who Lived in a Cave" in *Children of Wax: African Folktales* by Alexander McCall Smith (New York: Interlink Books, 1989) p. 11-17.

Smith collected this variant from a child in Zimbabwe, the country of his own birth and childhood. This variant begins with a girl being followed by a cannibal. When her family wants to move to avoid him the girl refuses to leave the area. She hides in a nearby cave and her brother brings her food each day. The cannibal soon alters his voice to match the brother's and tricks the girl into opening the cave. He takes her to his home, but just before the cannibal is able to cook and devour her, the brother knocks the cannibal into the fire. The flaming cannibal runs off and the entire family returns to the original home.

A Father's Children (Kamba: Kenya)

Retold from "The Father and the Children in the Eimu's Wilderness" in *Kamba Folklore II. Tales of Supernatural Beings and Adventures* by Gerhard Lindblom. Arches D'Etudes Orientales 20:2 (Lund: Berlingska Boktryckeriet, 1935).

Lindblom collected this variant while working in east Africa in 1912.

The Kamba are one of the four largest ethnic groups in the area of African now called Kenya. Though they moved about a great deal in the eighteenth and nineteenth centuries, the Kamba have traditionally been an agricultural people. They specialize in growing millet and sweet potatoes, often with the help of irrigation. Now mostly located southeast of Nairobi the Kamba people are also known for their woodcarving, ironsmith work, and traveling great distances to trade goods. They occasionally stay in tree huts to keep them safe from animals when they work as guards to protect the fields at night. English and Swahili are the official languages of Kenya.

Kamba lore features two kinds of eimu or spirit creatures. One kind comes from people who have died. The second kind comprises an ongoing parallel world that is a copy of the real world. These eimu live in houses just like people, have families, and raise crops. They also lurk everywhere and love to kill and eat real people. There are a few, however, some stories say, that become friendly and even marry humans.

Related variants

"The Story of the Old Man and His Knee" in *The Masai: Their Language and Folklore* by A.C. Hollis (Oxford: Clarendon Press, 1905) p. 153-55.

In this variant the man's children are kidnapped by one of his enemies. The father tracks down the villain and his children, but he is killed by angry neighbors when he cries out for his children. The children remain in the house of the enemy/villain.

"The Grandmother and the Apes" (Baganda: Uganda)

Reprinted from *Wakaima and the Clay Man and Other African Folk Tales* by E. Balintuma Kalibala and Mary Gould Davis (New York: Longmans Green, 1946).

Kalibala, a member of the Baganda people, heard this tale when he was a child living northwest of Lake Victoria in the early twentieth century. The ape in this tale resembles the eimu in the Kamba version, "A Father's Children." Both the ape and the eimu instruct the hero who kills them how to bring back to life all the others they have devoured.

Kalibala's tribe is one of 40 that now make up the nation of Uganda. Though tribal rivalries were common, local kingdoms and royal families lasted for hundreds of years. The area also has a history of being a meeting place of migrating cultures.

Arabs first visited the area in the 1840s, and Europeans followed in the 1870s. In 1893 England claimed the area and many people were forced to give up their fertile lands. Though Uganda gained its independence in 1962, it remains a land of political and military unrest. English and Swahili are the official languages.

Related Variants

"Nsangi" in *Songs and Stories from Uganda* by W. Moses Serwadda. Translated and edited by Hewitt Panteleoni (New York: Crowell, 1974) p. 45-51.

In this variant an ape tricks a girl into opening her door. Her mother finds and rescues her by questioning a group of 10 gorillas. When she finds the guilty ape she cuts off the little finger of his left hand and her daughter, Nsangi, is freed. Panteleoni states that this is probably the best-known story among the Baganda. Music is included for the mother's song.

The Three Kids (Cape Verde Islands)

Reprinted from *Folk-Lore from the Cape Verde Islands*, Part I, by Elsie Clews Parsons (Memoirs of the American Folk-Lore Society, Vol. 15:1) Cambridge, MA: American Folklore Society, 1923).

In 1916 and 1917 Parsons collected tales from Portuguese-African immigrants from Cape Verde, then living in New England. The teller of this tale was Jesufin Lopes, formerly of the Island of Fogo in the Cape Verde archipelago.

Cape Verde is located in the Atlantic Ocean 400 miles west of Senegal. It was uninhabited when claimed by Portugal in the fifteenth century. Portugal sent many settlers there, including a high percentage of convicts, and later imported black Africans for both free and slave labor. Because of its location, Cape Verde became a stopping place for many explorers and slave ships. Vasco de Gama stopped during his 1497 expedition, as did Amerigo Vespucci, Magellan, and Francis Drake at later dates. There were also times Cape Verde was attacked by pirates. Although Cape Verde was involved in slavery, there were also many freed and self-liberated slaves there. In the 1830s whaling ships began recruiting workers, and many

Cape Verde men immigrated to the United States with these jobs. Some stayed, while others later returned to their homeland. Since then many more, like the teller of this tale, have immigrated to New England to join their ancestors. Widespread intermarriage has made Cape Verde a truly multinational culture.

The Little She-Goat (Palestinian-Arab)

Reprinted from *Speak, Bird, Speak Again: Palestinian Arab Folktales* edited by Ibrahim Muhawi and Sharif Kanaana (Berkeley: University of California Press, 1989).

This tale was collected between 1978 and 1980 from a 55-year-old housewife named Fatme. She lived in Galilee in the village of Arrabe and had never lived more than 20 yards from the house of her birth. Though 11 of her 20 children survived, she was not usually a storyteller. Palestinian women are traditionally the tellers of animal tales, and with the collectors' children present, Fatme found she had many tales to share.

The land and people of Palestine share a long history of conflict and change. Until 70 A.D. when the Roman Empire destroyed their cities, the Jews had made Palestine their home. The people known as Palestinians are Muslims of mixed Arabic origins. At the beginning of the twentieth century Palestinians were the predominant population in Palestine and Jews were small in number. As Jews began to immigrate back to their ancient homeland the percentages gradually changed until the Palestinians became the minority. When the Jewish state of Israel was established by the United Nations in 1948 thousands of Palestinians found their lives turned upside down. There have been harsh feelings and ongoing battles between the Palestinians and Jews ever since. Over a million Palestinians are still living in Israel. At least another million are scattered and living as refugees.

Muhawi and Kanaana state that this general plot is so popular with Palestinians that it is included in almost every Palestinian collection of tales. There are Arabic variants in Egypt, Tunisia, Morocco, and Iraq that include the cumulative plot of "The Little She Goat." Other variants exist throughout the Arabian peninsula. Three variants from this area are included in this collection: "The Story of the Wolf and the Goat" (Kermani: Iran), "The Jackal and the Lambs" (Kabyl: Algeria), and "The Ewe, the Goat and the Lion" (Kurdistani-Jew).

Related Variants

"The Goat and the Ghoul" in "Palestinian Animal Stories and Fables" by Stephan H. Stephan. *Journal of the Palestinian Oriental Society* 3(1923): 167-71.

This variant was collected before 1923 when the Palestinians were still the dominant population in the area. A ghoul is the villain rather than a hyena, but the cumulative subplot of trying to get help altering a tail is the same as in "The Little She-Goat."

Variants of the "Chain" Tale Type 2034 ("The Mouse Regains Its Tale") include *One Fine Day*, retold by Nonny Hogrogian (New York: Macmillan, 1971).

The Golden Chain from Heaven (Japan)

Reprinted from *Folktales of Japan* edited by Keigo Seki. Translated by Robert J. Adams (Chicago: University of Chicago Press, 1963).

This tale was collected before 1956 from Kozo Nakano on the island of Shikoku. Scholarly research in Japanese folklore did not begin until 1910, but tales were included in other writings as early as the eighth century. A 31-volume collection of stories was published in the twelfth century and included many tales from India and China, as well as Japan. *Tales of Old Japan* by A.B. Mitford was the first volume published in English. Today folklorists have cited over 35 Japanese variants of this tale. Most of them have been found in the southern Kyushu Island area, which is near Korea.

The moon, which plays a vital role in this variant, has long been an important image in Japanese culture. In times past people gathered in parks and built platforms specially for moon-viewing, which was an artful custom accompanied by fine food and drink.

Though the Japanese have experienced many drastic changes, their culture and language have changed very little in the last 2,000 years. Chinese culture entered Japan during the fifth century by way of Korea. Portuguese traders reached Japan in the sixteenth century with Spain, the Netherlands, and Great Britain following closely behind. In its effort to avoid being colonized Japan closed its doors and borders to Europeans in the late 1600s. Japanese living outside of Japan at that time were not allowed to return, and those at home were not allowed to cross Japanese borders. It remained in isolation until the 1850s when the United States demanded relations and trade. This began a period of Japanese imperialism that continued till Japan's defeat in World War II. For the first seven years after World War II Japan was occupied by the U.S. forces. Today Japan is a leading country with strong international trade. Shintoism and Buddhism are the predominant religions.

The Sun and the Moon (Korea)

Reprinted from *Folktales from Korea* by Zong In-Sob (London: Routlege & Kegan Paul, 1952. Reprint. New York: Grove Press, 1979).

Inspired by W.B. Yeats' work with Irish folklore, Zong In-Sob began gathering folktales while still a college student. Both Yeats and Zong In-Sob believed publishing local folktales would enhance cultural pride. Zong In-Sob had heard many tales from his mother, sister, and classmates as a child growing up in the southwest farming area of Korea. This tale was collected from O Hwa-Su in 1911 and first published in 1927 in a Japanese collection of Korean tales called *Ondoru Yawa* (Korean Nights).

Korea is a geographical and cultural bridge linking China and Japan, and as a result, it is often the sight of conflicts. Korea has been under the rule of China, Japan, Mongolia, the U.S.S.R., and the United States. Even so, Korea has managed to maintain and nurture its unique culture. Korean states or kingdoms slowly developed in the first century, and by the fourth century, most people had converted to Buddhism. During the fifteenth

century Korea thrived in science, art, and technology, including the invention of a Korean alphabet.

Portuguese Christian missionaries entered Korea by way of China during the seventeenth and eighteenth centuries, and contact with Europeans increased throughout the 1800s. In 1910 Korea was made a Japanese colony.

During this period Japan tried to force Koreans to give up their language and their Korean names. When World War II ended with Japan's defeat, jurisdiction for Korea was divided between the United States and the Soviet Union. This eventually led to the division of the country into North and South Korea and the battles of the Korean conflict in the early 1950s. Korea remains a divided land of beauty and political tensions.

Related Variants

"The Sun, Moon and Stars" in *Korean Folk Tales* edited by International Cultural Foundation (Seoul: Si-sa-yong-o-sa, 1982) p. 29-32.

In this variant the children escape to become the sun, moon, and stars.

"The Three Little Girls" in *The Story Bag: A Collection of Korean Folktales* by Kim So-Un. Translated by Setsu Jigashi (Rutland, VT: Tuttle, 1955) p. 76-82.

The children test the character knocking at the door by voice, hands, and eyes. The three girls escape to become the sun, moon, and stars.

The Lame Wolf (Rajasthan/India)

Reprinted from *Folk Tales of Rajasthan* retold by Kamini Dinesh (Jodhpur, India: Jainsons Publications, 1979).

Dinesh worked from the text of Shri Vijai Dan Detha titled *Batan re Phulwadi*.

Rajasthan is the second largest state in India and located in the northwestern section, bordering Pakistan. It is a land of sun, sand, hills, and forests. Bright colored birds such as peacocks and parakeets are common. Once a land of kings or *maharajas*, this area still has forts that date back to the twelfth through fifteenth centuries. Though a large portion of Rajasthan is desert, other areas farm wheat and millet. Because of its size and history of battles the people of Rajasthan worship a wide range of religions. Hindu is predominant, but there are also many Muslims, Jains, and Sikhs. A small percentage of the population is Christian. India is such a large country that Rajasthan is closer to Afghanistan, Iran, and China than it is to the southern and eastern sections of India. The houses of most people in rural areas resemble the one deer builds in "The Lame Wolf"—mudwalls and a straw room with one door.

Related Variants

"The Girl and the Tiger-Man" (Manipur) in this collection.

Stith Thompson and Warren Roberts cite a variant in their:

Types of Indic Oral Tales: India, Pakistan and Ceylon (Folk Lore Fellows Communications #180, 1960): *Folktales from India* by M. N. Venkataswami (Madras, 1923) p. 114.

In this variant a crow teaches her four young ones not to open the door unless she calls their names. Their enemy overhears, calls their names, and eats them once they open the door.

The Monkey and the Hyena (Ngoni: Malawi)

Reprinted from *The Long Grass Whispers* by Geraldine Elliot (New York: Schocken, [1939] 1968).

Elliot collected this tale while living in the tropical area south of what was then called Lake Nyasa, the third largest lake in Africa. The preface to Elliot's sequel, *Where the Leopard Passes* (1949), refers to the tales being from the Ngoni people. Originally living farther to the south, the Ngoni migrated north into Malawi during the 1800s in an effort to escape troubled Zulu rule. Only the skeleton of this tale, however, is truly of the Ngoni. Elliott's writing style is elaborate and has little in common with traditional Ngoni storytelling.

Portuguese visited the area as early as 1616. Like Kenya and the west coast of Africa, the people of Malawi were hard hit by the slave trade.

The most famous European visitor to the area was Scottish abolitionist David Livingstone, who made four journeys there before 1863. After gaining their independence from Great Britain in 1964, the local peoples renamed the lake and their country Malawi.

Related Variants

"C'est Bouki, mon chère mari!" in *Tales from the French Folk-Lore of Missouri* by Joseph Medard Carriere (Evanston, IL: Northwestern University, 1937) p. 23-24.

An older couple decide they would rather live alone so they build a tree house for their three daughters to live in. The father takes them food each day and sings a certain song to tell them to drop down the rope. The supernatural bouki hears and tricks the girls. When the mother finds her daughters dead she tracks down the bouki and cuts his throat with a razor.

Jamaica Anansi Stories by Martha Warren Beckwith (Memoirs of the American Folk-Lore Society, Vol. 17) (New York: American Folk-Lore Society, 1924.)

This collection contains four brief variants on pages 20-22:

"Carencro's House with a Key." Liver is the key to crow's house and he calls for it to open the door. Hanansi hears him and tricks his way into the house.

"Duppy's House in the Air." Bre Duppy (the devil) makes a house in the air and goes and comes by way of a rope. Bredder Nansi tries to copy his actions.

"House in the Air." Anansi lives in a tree with his wife and children. Tiger and Bredder Tocoomah dog try to get pulled up the rope to their food supply.

"Rabbit and Children Going Up to Heaven." Rabbit and his children are pulled up to heaven to eat when "Mammy and Harry" pull up the rope. Brar Anansi tries to copy their voice and get their food.

Other related variants are discussed in notes for "When a Wise Man Dies, a Wise Man Buries Him."

Journey to the Mending City (Hausa: Nigeria)

Retold from "The Mender of Men" in *Hausa Superstitions and Customs: An Introduction to the Folklore and the Folk* by A.J.N. Tremearne (London: John Bale, 1913).

Hausa cities traditionally included a series of walled sections with large entrance gates. The mother's entrance into the city in "Journey to the Mending City" would have been a powerful scene. Houses were and are constructed of pear-shaped mud bricks coated with more mud compounds, then carved and painted with rich textures and designs. House designs range from the simplicity of adobe shapes to palaces with vaulted roots that resemble cathedrals. Hausaland included seven major cities with dense populations. Each city had numerous, smaller satellite villages. For more background on the Hausa please see notes for "The Water of Ladi."

Related Variants

Variants of Tale Type 480, or "The Kind and Unkind Girls," include:

"Mother Holle" in *The Complete Grimms' Fairy Tales* (New York: Pantheon, 1944) p. 133-36.

The Talking Eggs: A Folktale from the American South retold by Robert D. San Soucci. Illustrated by Jerry Pinkney (New York: Dial, 1989).

The Tongue-Cut Sparrow retold by Momoko Ishi. Translated by Katerine Paterson. Illustrated by Seukichi Akaba (New York: Dutton, 1982).

Indesoka (Madagascar)

Retold from "Indesoka, Child of Itrimobe" in "The Oratory, Songs, Legends and Folk-Tales of the Malagsy" by James Sibtree, Jr. *Folk-Lore Journal* 1(1883): 273-77.

Though Madagascar is geographically closer to southeast Africa, its people and culture are closer to those of Asia. The first inhabitants of Madagascar are believed to have migrated from Indonesia over two thousand years ago. Swahili-speaking Muslims from northeast Africa came next. Over time people from India, Pakistan, and China migrated to this archipelago in the Indian Ocean. Eventually 18 subgroups of the Malagasy people developed. Europe became aware of Madagascar in the sixteenth century as it searched for slaves and settlements. The British were influential in Madagascar for some time, but the Merina monarchs had almost unified the state when the French took over and made Madagascar their colony late in the nineteenth century. The language of Madagascar is a Malagasy mixture of all immigrant languages. Today, French, English and Merina (a dialect of Malagasy) are the dominant languages. Much of Madagascar is as unique to the world as "Indesoka" is to this collection. Plants and animals found nowhere else in the world thrive in Madagascar's tropical climate. These include over 40 kinds of lemurs, a primate that resembles a blend of monkey and cat.

Related Variants

"Indesoka, Child of Intrimobe" in *Specimens of Malagasy Folklore* by Lars Dahle (Antananarivo: A. Kingdon, 1887).

French language variants can be traced through:

Malagasy Tale Index by Lee Harding (Folk Lore Fellows Communications #231, 1982).

African Folk Tales with Foreign Analogues by May Augusta Klipple. Dissertation (Indiana University, 1938).

The Tiger Witch (Taiwan)

Reprinted from *Tales from a Taiwan Kitchen* by Cora Cheney (New York: Dodd, Mead & Co, 1976).

Cora Cheney collected this variant from the Ho family near Taipei while she was teaching English writing in Taiwan. It is different from most Chinese variants because it includes a father and explains his absence.

The people and folklore of the mountainous island nation Taiwan reflect several cultures. The indigenous Malayo-Polynesian people were first visited by the Chinese during the thirteenth century. Immigration continued, and by the seventeenth century large numbers of people were immigrating from the Fukien Province in China. The Portuguese were the first Europeans to visit Taiwan near the end of the sixteenth century. The Dutch soon followed. Spain offered some competition in colonizing the island, but by the middle of the seventeenth century the Dutch were the only Europeans on Taiwan. After the Sino-Japanese War in 1895, Japan took control of Taiwan until the end of World War II. Japan worked hard to prohibit the Chinese language and culture but much survived, including folktales. A new wave of immigrants entered Taiwan in 1949 during the Communist revolution that created the People's Republic of China.

Related Variants

"The Chinese Red Riding Hoods" told by Isabelle Chang in *Womenfolk and Fairy Tales* edited by Rosemary Minard (Boston: Houghton Mifflin, 1975) p. 14-19.

This variant begins with the epigraph "Beware of the wolf in sheep's clothing." The wolf pretends to be the grandmother and the three girls let him in. He blows out the candles so he can hide in the darkness. The girls save themselves by climbing the gingko tree.

Lon Po Po: A Red-Riding Hood Story from China translated and illustrated by Ed Young (New York: Philomel, 1989).

This is an outstanding picturebook edition of the standard Chinese tale and somewhat less graphic than "The Tiger Witch."

The Girl and the Tiger-Man (Manipur: India)

Retold from "Kabui-Keioiba" in *Folktales of Nagaland, Manipur, Tripura and Mizoram* by B.K. Borgohain and P.C. Roy Chadbury (New Delhi: Sterling, 1975).

Manipur is located in far eastern India along the Burmese border and is relatively isolated. Being neighbors of Burma, the two have often battled and at times Manipur has been occupied by the Burmese. The Manipuri language is part of the Tibeto-Burman family. There is little written history of the area before the nineteenth century, when Hindus began to immigrate to the area. In 1948 Manipur became a part of the Republic of India. The dominant valley in the country is surrounded by hills that include 12 different tribes and languages that make up half the state's population. Contemporary Manipuri folklore still refers to a Tiger-man creature like that in "The Girl and the Tiger-Man" as living in the eastern hills. Manipur is the home of the only one of India's seven classic dances in which men and women dance together. The Manipuri version of "The Knock at the Door" is also one of the few to feature a victimized female saving herself.

The Goat and the Kids and the Bogey (Embu: Kenya)

Reprinted from *The Vanishing Tribes of Kenya* by Major G. St. J. Orde-Browne (London: Seeley, 1925. Reprint, Westport, CT: Negro Universities Press, 1970).

Orde-Browne collected this tale from an older woman during his research between 1909 and 1916. On many occasions he was the first European his tellers had seen.

The Embu, similar in culture to the Mbeere, are among the least populous peoples out of the 30 ethnic groups that make up Kenya. They live and farm on the southern slope of Mt. Kenya, north of the Kamba people. The Embu experienced very little European influence until the early twentieth century. Long before Europeans began settling, however, Swahili slave traders from the coast near Zanzibar ventured into Embu lands to kidnap people as slaves. Embu villages tend to be smaller than other neighboring cultures and more freely arranged. The door the villain tricks the kids into opening is likely made of woven wicker or thin twigs. Goats are raised for eating (not milk) and used for all ceremonies.

Essays and Resources

One Tale around the World

Though all the tales in *A Knock at the Door* share a common story there are few simple or singular answers to the questions "What happens?" and "What's it about?" All the tales share a knock at the door after characters have been warned not to open the door to strangers. Most of the tales also feature a villain impersonating a family member or friend to get inside the house. But before and after the knock at the door these tales are as variegated as a garden of lilies. Of the two questions, "What happens?" is the easier to answer. Characters and plot can be listed and mapped. "What's it about?" is a matter of theme and emotion, elements as open to interpretation as asking "Which lily in the garden is best?"

Answers to both questions are affected by the driving question of any story—"What if?" In fable form the story has little action or plot. The mother goat says "Don't open the door," and the little kid does not. All is well. But what if he did? What if the kid was as smart as he could be and *still* got fooled? What if he got devoured? *Then* what would the mother do?

How Did These Variants Evolve?

Not all variants grew out of Aesop's fable, the oldest version of this tale, though many surely did. It is likely, however, that all variants grew out of these questions being asked in response to the universal protective warning, "Don't open the door to strangers." As these questions have been answered again and again, new stories evolved from old.

Some of the questions that built these tales are sparked by historical events and a culture's particular view of the world. Other questions and, thus, changes to these tales, come about from people's need to explain how the world as it is came to be. Some variants were likely sparked by a teller's dream long ago and others from other stories.

Tales travel no matter what the goal of the journey—imperialism, migration, enslavement, missionary zeal, education reform, or refugees seeking safety. A rapid look through a historical atlas becomes a violent dance of lines, and for every change in a line, people have been affected. Virtually every culture represented in *A Knock at the Door* has, at some time, lived the role of the wolf sweet-talking, then forcing its way into another's home and devouring what it found. And just as often, these same cultures have lived the role of the littlest kid hiding during times of dominance and destruction in hopes that home can be reborn once the wolf gets tired and lazy. Germany has been the wolf to France while France has been the wolf to Madagascar. Korea to Japan and Japan to Korea. The list is long. After Spain lived the role of the seventh little kid while Rome, France, and the Moors played wolf, it later played wolf to West Africa and the Americas. The desire to dominate other cultures, homes, and lands seems as deeply ingrained in humankind as its need to share stories and warn, "Don't open the door!" Jews and Palestinians share this story, as do Germans and Jews. So do Iran and Iraq, the United States and Iraq, and Iraq and the Kurdish refugees. North Americans with African, Asian, and European roots all share the story, too, like both sides of South Africa's apartheid wall.

Tracing the Roots of Folktales

For some scholars exploring the history of a folktale is a fascinating puzzle that involves tracing a tale's geographic journey. People are forever exploring and migrating (by choice or force), and stories go wherever people go. Others scholars believe tales that are similar began spontaneously in different parts of the world. The truth—as in most situations—is most likely a blend of both perspectives. It is unlikely that all 35 versions of "The Knock at the Door" tale included here grew from the same initial tale. Some simultaneity surely occurred, but we also know of specific cases where tales did travel. "The Rabbit and the Bear" (Pennsylvania Dutch: U.S.), for example, migrated with the Germans who came to North America in the eighteenth century. The Cape Verde version, "The Three Kids," did not exist in Cape Verde until Europeans and Africans settled the deserted islands. And, the Cape Verde tale included in this collection was collected from a man who had moved from Cape Verde to the United States.

Tracing a tale's journey can personalize history's places and dates, but it can also easily degenerate into a game of cultural chauvinism of "we were first" and "first is best." It is only recently, for example, that the European bias has been challenged in the classic tale type and motif indexes. Early theories that all African tales with European variants had to have come *from* Europe are now being disproven.

Ultimately, the genealogy of a tale goes beyond time, race, boundaries, and flags to the essential source of both the tale *and* its perpetuation—the human condition. The seed for all the tales in *A Knock at the Door* is humanity's dual longing for safety and story—the heart of the latter being conflict and risk.

What do Folktales Mean?

Even when told as a fable, various tellers have assigned different morals in response to the question, "What's it about?" Many say the story is about the importance of obeying one's mother. Marie de France's eleventh-century retelling is not so much about obeying mother as watching out for bad advice and the evils of feigning truth. Roger L'Estrange's interpretation from the seventeenth century found the tale to be about "There never was any hypocrite so disguis'd, but he had some mark or other yet to be known by."

Expanded to a dramatic folktale, the tale's range of themes grows wider when the kids open the door. Looking at only the German variant, "The Wolf and the Seven Little Kids," Erich Franzke (Franzke, 1985, 75) shares some of the distilled answers his clients have found to the question, "What's it about?"

Moral meanings:
- A mother should never leave her children.
- Children should never let a stranger in.
- One learns only by experiencing danger personally.
- The smallest has it best.

Metaphoric meanings:
- The old nanny goat represents well-intentioned, but unfounded admonitions.
- The nanny goat's departure makes developmental progress possible.
- The wolf represents confrontation with greed, with cleverness, and with unchecked fulfillment of desire.

At times, changes in characters and/or plot affect the story's theme or add an additional layer of meaning to those above. The Czecho-Slovak variant as told by Bozena Nemcova, "Four Disobedient Kids," is in part about the dangers of inner-family fighting. A Hausa variant, "Journey to the Mending City," explores the errors of mimicking another's behavior. A variant with human characters from Grenada, "Devil Hammers His Tongue," is about the evil of loving one child more than another. An extended Haitian version of this same variant (see notes for "Devil Hammers His Tongue") grows in plot to become a tale about the beauty of forgiveness.

What the tale is about must never be confined to simple answers or the morals attached to fable variants. More than anything else tales are emotional experiences, feelings evoked for the pleasure and contemplation of both teller and audience. As actor Jack Nicholson has said about acting, the role of the tale and the teller is a "stimulating point of departure . . . what you're supposed to do is keep people vitally interested in the world they live in . . . to make people, not necessarily happy, but enrich their vitality" (Nicholson, 1986, 48).

The Characters and Their Roles

Answers to the question, "What happens in the tale?" becomes a walk through a global garden of seemingly endless varieties. At the tale's outermost edges are the changes in characters who play the roles of parent, child, and villain; or mother goat, kid, and wolf. Anthropomorphic animals take these roles according to natural behavior. The rabbits of the Pennsylvania Dutch variant are threatened by a bear. Hyenas threaten monkeys in the Ngoni/Malawi variant. And, East Indian deer and Kabyl/Algerian lambs are both threatened by a jackal.

Other cultures and variants feature animals or people battling supernatural villains. In Spain the little goats are tricked by the wild monster, Carlanco, instead of a wolf. Japanese children battle Carlanco's kindred evil spirit, Yamauba. The Kamba of Kenya must battle a spirit figure called the eimu while the Embu of Kenya are devoured by the female Bogey. In Vanuatu a good spirit figure, Tagaro, matches wits with another spirit, the evil and shapeless Mera-mbuto.

As in daily life, age alone does not define one's role within a family. In the Yiddish-Canadian variant, "A Granny Who Had Many Children," the grandmother rescues young children from the bear. In contrast, "The Grandmother and the Apes" (Baganda: Uganda) reverses the roles and the children rescue the grandmother. Almost all the variants of "When a Wise Man Dies" (Cameroon) feature children in the protective role and mothers as the ones hidden for their protection.

Some variants divide the role of parent and child between two or more children left on their own. In "The Story of Demane and Demazana" (Xhosa: South Africa) and "The Water of Ladi" (Hausa: Nigeria) a brother acts as guardian to a sister and rescues her from the villain with the help of others. And like most children, Tagaro in "Tagaro's Fish" (Vanuatu) serves as parent/protector to his pet.

The genders of these roles are not rigid either. Females are not always rescued by males, nor are all villains male. Female villains knock at the door in "The Water of Ladi" (Hausa: Nigeria), "The Goat and the Kids and the Bogey" (Embu: Kenya), and "The Golden Chain from Heaven" (Japan). In the African-American variant, "The Cunning Snake," the one who knocks on the door is a female snake avenging the kidnapping/death of her own egg-child by the woman in the tale. "A Father's Children" (Kamba: Kenya) offers one of the most

interesting twists among the variants. A man out hunting with other men gives birth to children through a swollen place on his knee. Without question he nurtures them as a mother would do. The danger that knocks on his children's door is not a male in any form, but an ogress-like female called an eimu. "Father Found," a variant from the Bahamas (see notes for "Tiger Softens His Voice") features a father in the classic role of overprotective dad. His interest in hiding and protecting his daughter is to keep her away from men, but she isn't so sure she wants to be protected.

Humans rather than anthropomorphic goats play the child or victim in many variants but are rarely given the role of villain at the door. In "Indesoka" (Malagasy) the child's father has the wolf's role, but he is identified as an ogre rather than a man. The villain, who in the end wants to marry his victim in "The Girl and the Tiger-Man" (Manipur: India), can make himself look like a man, but that is not his true nature.

The Caribbean appears to be the one geographical area that features humans in all roles, but with this comes a major plot twist. The knock at the door is not always in search of supper. Sometimes the search is for love. "La Belle Venus" (Haiti) concludes with a joyful, romantic union between the young woman initially hidden away and the man who knocked at her door.

Recognizing one's mother's voice is an early point of assurance for babies, as well as mother's shape, touch, and smell. Those characters such as the wolf in "The Wolf and the Seven Little Kids" (German) who alter their voices and hands to match the mother's are the most villainous of all who come knocking on doors. They destroy the child's primary references to the world and safety.

The desire of these villains is so great that they will go through great pain and mutilation to succeed. The German wolf only has to eat chalk to sweeten his voice, and the ogre in "Indesoka" (Malagasy) changes his by eating a raw egg. The tiger and cannibal, however, in "Tiger Softens His Voice" (Jamaica) and "The Story of Demane and Demazana" (Xhosa: South Africa) both have to thrust hot pokers down their throats. Others have their tongues filed down. The jackal in "The Jackal and the Lambs" (Kabyl: Algeria) and the eimu in

"A Father's Children" (Kamba: Kenya) sweeten their voices by having ants and scorpions bite their tongues. The wolf in "The Three Kids" (Cape Verde Islands) sits in a cooking pot of hot water for three days to alter his voice. A few are lucky enough to find pills or some form of magic to help, but failing to follow strict instructions can undo the change in voice. Hyena in "Journey to the Mending City" (Hausa: Nigeria) must have his voice altered a second time because his greed gets him in trouble. The Tiger-man in "The Girl and the Tiger-Man" (Manipur: India) threatens an old woman into using her voice to trick the girl and open the door.

These villains know what they want and they want it *now*. Patience is clearly not one of their virtues. Only a few like the snake in "The Cunning Snake" (African-American: U.S.) are crafty and patient enough to practice until they get the words and voice just right.

The words themselves are the key point of recognition in many variants, serving much like an extended password. One of La Fontaine's rich touches in his fable retelling is to make the passwords a statement against wolves. In order for the wolf to trick the kid into opening the door he has to speak words condemning himself. On the one hand it's a comic scene—a villain lambasting himself. On the other hand, it's even more villainous. The wolf becomes the slick-talking heel who tells his date how most men are so childishly sex-minded and disrespectful of women as part of his own seduction scheme.

Variants that center around passwords or songs rather than voice are not necessarily less personal than others—merely different. In the Caribbean, for example, where songs are believed to have magical powers, a song is often the key to opening the door. The voice of the singer may not matter so much because the song itself evokes so much power.

The Plots

Plot lines offer a greater range of differences among variants even when the characters remain the same. A few variants answer the question, "What if the kids opened the door?" by allowing the wolf inside and then foiling his efforts. The kids in "The Goat, the Kids and the Wolf" (France) trick the wolf into a storage space and keep him locked up till their mother returns. In Spain the monster Carlanco tricks his way into the house but can't get into the tiny attic where the kids run to hide.

A few kids are not so fortunate and live the darker side of the fable. In "The Goat and the Kids" (Mordvin: Russia) the kids are tricked into opening the door and when the mother returns they've all been devoured. All she can do is grieve. The kids in the Czecho-Slovak variant as told by Bozena Nemcova are devoured after knocking the door open themselves by accident. The human mother in "The Devil Hammers His Tongue" (Grenada) has no means to regain the two daughters she lost and must learn to love the one she has left.

Few of the mothers or fathers, however, are willing to settle for grief. Even if their lost children cannot be rescued, revenge or retribution is sought. The ewe in "The Jackal and the Lambs" (Kabyl: Algeria) cannot save her lambs, but she can destroy the jackal. When she sees him one day the ewe covers him with hay and sits on him, calling out to a shepherd. When the shepherd hears what the jackal has done, he beats the jackal to death.

The majority of variants end on a happier note. The parental figure becomes as omnipresent as the mother in *The Runaway Bunny* by Margaret Wise Brown and Clement Hurd. Water and fire, two primary needs for survival (in addition to mothers), bring survival to the kids at the same time they bring the wolf's demise. In the well-known German variant, "The Wolf and the Seven Little Kids," the wolf is cut open, filled with stones, and then drowns. The kids in many Russian variants are freed when the wolf falls while jumping over a fire and explodes.

With folktales being one of society's ways of affirming morals and manners it is not surprising that characters who deceitfully knock on the door have trouble finding help. Many do get help, but most often through violent means. The grieving parent, however, finds many others ready to help rescue the children.

The mother in "The Rabbit and the Bear" (Pennsylvania Dutch: U.S.) gathers a parade of helping animals. After the wasps sting the bear, making him run out of the house, all the other animals attack him and knock him down the hill. In

One Tale around the World

"Carlanco" (Spain) the story opens with the mother goat rescuing a wasp out of the goodness of her heart. Later, when her children are cornered by the monster, the wasp returns the favor by stinging Carlanco till he runs away. The child victim in "The Story of Demane and Demazana" (Xhosa: South Africa) is rescued by her brother and bees. Though she initially has problems finding someone brave enough for the task, the mother goat in "The Three Kids" (Cape Verde Islands) regains her children with the vital help of an ant.

"The Water of Ladi" (Hausa: Nigeria) involves helpful creatures along with a bit of blackmail and social judgment. The victim's protector steals the water from the pond and refuses to return it until the hyena has returned his sister. Eventually the animals get so thirsty they attack the hyena. In the fight the lion tears open the hyena, and the girl is freed.

A slightly more formal process of help and judgment appears in "The Ewe, the Goat and the Lion" (Kurdistani-Jew). The grieving ewe charges several animals with killing her children. When she charges the lion he insists they see a judge. After the lion's bribe backfires the judge pulls out the lion's teeth, sharpens the ewe's horns and orders them to fight it out. The ewe easily gores the lion and frees her children.

Two variants from the area of Lake Victoria— "A Father's Children" (Kamba: Kenya) and "The Grandmother and the Apes" (Baganda: Uganda)— include a morally ambiguous character that seems to have no sense of right or wrong. First these characters help the villain capture the victim and then they help the parental figure rescue the same victim. If they were paid for their actions and advice these characters would simply be greedy and troublesome. Unpaid, as they are, they bring up prickly questions of who deserves help when, and when does helping become an evil act?

In some variants the kids themselves help the villain while trying to help themselves. The kids are so eager to establish their comparative knowledge they naively help the wolf. Rather than just saying "Go away" or "Your voice is not the right voice" they give the wolf the information he needs in impersonate their mother and fool them. "Your voice is rough. Our mother's is soft and sweet." "Your paws are too dark. Our mother's paws are soft and white." Simply by following their directions, the wolf is able to trick them into opening the door and the kids are so sure of their wisdom they don't think twice.

As most people eventually learn, one's parents can't protect or rescue them from everything. Four variants in A Knock at the Door feature children who save themselves from danger. The monkey left at home to babysit in "The Monkey and the Hyena" (Ngoni: Malawi) is never fooled by hyena. When another monkey later falls for hyena's trick the first monkey bites through the rope and saves his family. Filled with new respect for him, his family makes the first monkey their new leader. The children in "The Tiger Witch" (Taiwan) save themselves from being devoured and tell their mother the whole story when she returns the next day. The young woman in "The Girl and the Tiger-Man" (Manipur: India) who is kidnapped knows her brothers are looking for her, but she doesn't want to wait. While the Tiger-man has an old woman lie at the beginning of the tale to help him get inside the girl's house, the girl lies later on. Her impersonation of love and friendship tricks the beastly Tiger-man into revealing too much of himself, including the one way he can be killed. The girl is so effective at rescuing herself that she is already on her way home when she meets her seven brothers coming to help her.

When the Bogey tricks her way into the goat's home in "The Goat and the Kids and the Bogey" (Embu: Kenya) she eats only the three youngest kids. The fourth and oldest saves himself by promising to become her slave. It takes patience and planning, but the young goat eventually succeeds. When he has acquired the strength needed to kill the Bogey he does, cuts her open, and frees his siblings. This variant has an unusually cyclical ending. When the kids return to their home and knock on the door their mother won't let them in at first. Her kids, she tells them, have been devoured by the Bogey so they must be imposters.

In contrast to variants that feature self-saving children is "The Goat and the Wolf" (Afghanistan), which all but deletes the victims as characters. It begins like most other versions with the mother leaving her children at home, but it distills the core drama of the knock at the door into two sentences: "One day the mother went out to look for food for her children. While she was gone a wolf stole into her house and gobbled up all three children." The plot then leaps forward to the mother's return, how she takes revenge, and saves her children. Like the goat in "The Story of the Wolf and the Goat" (Kermani: Iran) and the ewe in "The Ewe, the Goat, and the Lion" (Kurdistani-Jew), this mother gains help by giving a gift. In exchange for food the blacksmith sharpens her horns. The wolf gives the blacksmith a bogus gift, causing him to pull out the wolf's teeth rather than sharpen them. When the goat and wolf fight, the goat easily wins, and when her sharp horns gore the wolf, her three kids are set free.

Significant Plot Variations

A handful of variants have narratives that are significantly different in terms of plot. Some differences occur between the more typical points or chords of the story. Others are so different or elaborate they overlap plots of other well-known tales such as "Mother Holle," "The Juniper Tree," "Beauty and the Beast," and "Little Red Riding Hood."

"The Cunning Snake" (African-American: U.S.) contains a prestory. A woman out walking sees a snake's egg. After dreaming about it she returns, takes it, and immediately cooks it for breakfast. When the snake returns to her nest/home and finds her egg/child gone she tracks down the one who has devoured her child. The woman, like most villains in these tales, denies any knowledge of the missing child. Angry, the snake threatens revenge—a child for a child. When the woman later has *her* child, the snake's revenge begins and the snake's role evolves from the positive mother's role of losing a child to that of the deceitful villain.

The prestory for "The Lame Wolf" (Rajasthan/India) is more extended setting than plot. Deer has yet to have her children. Time and again she literally puts her life on the line for her future children by sitting on the road in hopes passers-by will give her materials to build a safe home. This variant also has a character or role unique to itself. The young deer are not kept from opening the door by *their* reasoning but because the saffron tree in their yard warns them not to. It is only after the wolf has uprooted and burned the tree to ashes that the young deer open the door.

Relationship of "A Knock at the Door" Tales to Other Tale Types

The Palestinian-Arab variant, "The Little She-Goat" contains a cumulative tale (type 2034) within its primary plot. When hyena wants to alter his tail to fool the goat he ends up going from character to character who each demand a favor before helping him. Each favor leads to the next as in *One Fine Day* by Nonny Hogrogian (Macmillan, 1971).

When the mother in "Journey to the Mending City" (Hausa: Nigeria) takes her daughter's remains to be mended the narrative expands into a variant of tale type 480 ("Kind and Unkind Girls") familiar to many in "Mother Holle" (German) and "The Tongue-Cut Sparrow" (Japan). Though offered self-cooking food several times along her journey, the mother refuses. Later, when told to tend the cattle while her daughter waits to be mended, the mother feeds the cattle the best of the fruit and only eats the bad herself. Her daughter is mended back to her original beauty. When a second mother (a second wife of the same husband) finds out, she purposely kills her daughter and sets out to echo the first mother's journey and success. But in every instance where the first mother had been generous, the second is greedy. As a result, the conclusion of this variant is not the mother's rescuing her child, but the punishment the second mother and daughter receive because of their greed and lack of individuality.

"Indesoka" (Malagasy) is even darker in theme and echoes the cannibalistic evil of "The Juniper Tree" (German) and the ancient myth of Kronos who devours his own children. The villain in "Indesoka" is the victim's ogre-father. After tricking his way into her hiding place he kills her and orders his wife to cook the meat for supper. Thanks to her mother's rejuvenating skills and secrecy the girl is reborn in a vessel. The mother's retribution matches the crime. She tricks and kills her ogre-husband and then serves him to his family as dinner.

A Roumanian variant (see notes for "The Wolf and the Goat") is more gentle in tone and action, but still contains a level of inner-family violence. When the wolf is first introduced in the story it is as the kid's godfather. Like Indesoka's father, this godfather wolf dismisses his parental responsibilities and sacrifices his own children to his gluttony and greed.

Many who read "The Girl and the Tiger-Man" (Manipur: India) will be reminded of "Beauty and the Beast." The young women in both tales find themselves captive to a beastly male who longs to be loved by them. "The Girl and the Tiger-Man," however, is far from being a romantic tale. This young woman proves to be as cunning as the villain. Her act of self-preserving revenge not only kills the Tiger-man but burns his house to the ground with her child fathered by him inside. As in "The Cunning Snake" (African-American: U.S.), the black and white roles of victim and villain are wrapped in gray by the end of this variant.

The perpetual confluence of folktales brings two more well-known tales to the edges of *A Knock at the Door*—"Little Red Riding Hood" and "The Three Little Pigs." In some ways, "Little Red Riding Hood" is the flip side of tale type 123, or "The Knock at the Door." Little Red Riding Hood leaves home to enter the safety of her grandmother's home only to encounter the wolf pretending to be an intimate family member. Perrault's version published in 1697 is the dark side of Aesop's coin. Where Aesop's kid cannot be fooled, Little Red Riding Hood is tricked and as a result is devoured.

The German variant, "Little Red Cap," perhaps the best-known variant in the United States, has even more in common with "The Wolf and the Seven Little Kids." Many scholars believe the Grimms grafted the happy ending of cutting open the wolf and filling him with stones onto "Little Red Riding Hood" to make it a more joyful tale.

Many Asian variants of "The Wolf and the Seven Little Kids" are also variants of "Little Red Riding Hood." "The Golden Chain from Heaven" (Japan), "The Sun and the Moon" (Korea), and "The Tiger-Witch" (Taiwan) all contain elements of both tales. They are included in *The Knock at the Door* because a villain pretending to be a family member tricks his or her way into the house. Once the villain is in the house these variants switch to the slower tension of "Little Red Riding Hood."

Recognition of the villain is slow and troublesome because of the lack of light. Unlike most variants, these three take place at night.

The overlapping of "The Three Little Pigs" and "The Wolf and the Seven Little Kids" seems to be more of an academic snarl than a reality of folklore. Stith Thompson connects or confuses the two in *The Folktale* (1946). Thompson identifies tale type 123 as "The Three Little Pigs" and describes the basic tale as "the adventure of the young animals—seven goats, three pigs, or the like—who are left at home by their mother in their house and warned not to open the door to the wolf" (Thompson, 1946, 39). However, the basic tale of "The Three Pigs" as told by Joseph Jacobs and others has the pigs leaving home, building houses, and having their doors blown down by a wolf. Thompson also identifies tale type 123 as "The Three Little Pigs" in *European Tales among the North American Indians* (1919). But the only element the Flathead tale he cites has in common with "The Wolf and the Seven Little Kids" is having a villain come to the door.

A.J.N. Treamearne also confuses the two tales in his collection, *Hausa Superstitions* (1913). Treamearne's note connects "Journey to the Mending City" with "The Three Little Pigs" as told by Joseph Jacobs, but there is no tangible similarity between the two tales. In his own notes for *English Fairy Tales* (1898) Joseph Jacobs suggests a possible connection between "The Wolf and the Seven little Kids" and "The Three Little Pigs" because of their chins. Jacobs believes the pigs' famous line "Not by the hair of my chinny chin chin" makes no sense for a hairless pig, but a goat with its beard could logically say the same line.

To date I have located only one partial example of a version of "The Three Little Pigs" containing a deceitful knock at the door. In *Nights With Uncle Remus* (1887) Joel Chandler Harris tells the "real" story of "The Three Little Pigs" titled "The Story of the Pigs." This version has five pigs who, just like those in other versions, leave home and build their own houses. The wolf blows his way inside the first three houses and devours the pigs. He tricks the fourth pig into letting him literally get a foot in the door, then devours the fourth pig. When the wolf reaches the last pig's house he alters his voice and pretends to be one of the sibling pigs he's already eaten. In his notes Harris connects this tale with "The Story of Demane and Demazana" (Xhosa: South Africa), which had been published in *Kaffir Folktales* (Theal 1886) the previous year.

What Is Lost When Tales Are Changed to Protect

On occasion those who publish written retellings go beyond style to alter plot, thus creating a secondary kind of variant. When the purpose of the retelling is to protect the child from folklore's metaphoric violence the changes made can leave the tale a shadow of its former self and shadow-thin. Lawton B. Evan's retelling, "Snowflake," in *Worthwhile Stories for Everyday* ([1917] 1928) is representative of such variants. The kid refuses to open the door to the wolf's voice and demands he show a foot in the door crack. The wolf flours his hand and is again rejected by the kid who explains his mother's hand is hard, not soft. Then the tale spins off in a completely new direction. When the wolf returns a third time and the kid asks, "Who's there?" the wolf echoes back, "Who's there?" The kid tells the wolf to show his foot. Then for no apparent reason the wolf sticks his soft tail through the crack in the door. The kid grabs it, ties it in a knot, and traps the wolf. The wolf's sudden and blatant stupidity keeps the kid from being devoured, but it also dilutes the drama of the story and the audience's involvement.

Two recent picturebook editions offer other alteration. *Mother Goose and the Sly Fox* by Chris Conover (Farrar, 1989) includes a tertiary character called a "Do-Nothing Mouse." Since Conover gives no sources for her retelling it is impossible to know if the mouse is her invention or a standard element in a variant not available in English. As with "Snowflake" the change in plot dilutes the drama of the tale. Though the mouse does little within the story's action his role turns the goslings into bystanders in their own story. It is the mouse who is in charge of opening the door and protecting the children, not the children/goslings themselves. Though the mouse fails at his duty Mother Goose rescues her goslings from the fox's sack. When she scolds the mouse for failing to do his duty, the mouse cooks them a delicious supper to "show that he could do things right."

Eric Kimmel's retelling, *Nanny Goat and the Seven Little Kids* (Holiday, 1990), offers another twist in the plot. The wolf not only swallows all seven kids, he swallows the mother when she returns. Devoured so quickly, the mother never really loses her children and never grieves. To be sure, the kids are upset at being in the wolf's stomach, but the mother is with them and thanks to her ever-handy sewing scissors she snips their way out. "Snowflake" has long since faded from view. Time will determine if these other literary variants sufficiently satisfy the audience's desire for entertainment and vicarious drama and take root in public memory.

Cultural Range of These Tales

The cultural range of the tales included in *A Knock at the Door* is readily apparent. The evolution of these variants and the simultaneity of their being told is far more difficult to discern and map. Oral literature does not need print to survive and grow, but the printed version of an oral tale is one of the few ways to trace its history.

Though Aesop never wrote down his fables, his reputation as a teller was noted in early Greek written literature. Historians place Aesop in the sixth century B.C. and a contemporary of the poet Sappho. The first written versions of his fables are attributed to the Greek scholar Demetrius in the fourth century B.C.

Phaedrus translated Aesop into Latin early in the first century A.D., and Babrius of the same period included "The Kid and the Wolf" in his versification of Aesop's fables. The next two notable editions or retellings of Aesop appeared in the Middle Ages during the last part of the twelfth century. Both have ties with France. Rabbi Berechiah ha-Nakdan, a French resident, has often been called the Jewish Aesop. Marie de France wrote her fables in French verse, but is believed to have been living in England at the time.

The first English and Spanish editions of Aesop and "The Kid and the Wolf" leap forward another two centuries. The British publisher Caxton produced an edition in 1484. A few years later *Ysopete Ystoriado* (1489) appeared in Spain.

The next and perhaps the last major retelling of Aesop occurred in the seventeenth century, proving the fable's continued popularity and vitality. Jean de La Fontaine's poetic retellings were composed between 1668 and 1694. They were so highly regarded and became so popular that children in France are as familiar with the fables as children in the United States are with Mother Goose rhymes.

The next leap in print for "The Kid and the Wolf" is in form and time. At some point the fable had begun to grow into a folktale of drama and adventure. Its first published appearance as a tale was in 1812 as "The Wolf and the Seven Little Kids" in *Kinder- und Hausmärchen* by the Brothers Grimm. The Grimms' research sparked worldwide interest in gathering folklore, and variants have since been found around the world.

Simultaneity, evolution, and endurance are three of folklore's strongest threads. To assume that all the variants in *A Knock at the Door* are still being told in the oral tradition would be naive. Print and electronic media have greatly altered the way folklore is shared. But whether a strong oral telling of the tale survives or not, people in various cultures may well be familiar with it, just as people in the United States are familiar with "Hansel and Gretel" even if they've never heard it told aloud. A tale loved by the masses will find its place in contemporary forms whether they are books, films, cartoons, or TV commercials.

One way to gain a sense of simultaneity, evolution, and endurance is to look at when the variants of a tale were collected in the field. Such dates, as listed below for the tales in *A Knock at the Door*, are clearly just the tip of a folkloric iceberg. Stith Thompson cites over 25 more non-English variants in *The Types of the Folktale* (1961).

The dates given in the chart below refer only to longer or nonfable versions of "The Knock at the Door," beginning with *Kinder- und Hausmärchen* collected by the Brothers Grimm. These dates also reflect the gradual broadening of folklore research from Europe to around the world as indicated by the larger number of non-Western tales collected in later years. Dates document when a variant was collected, but have *no* relationship to when that version may have been created.

Those who tell a tale to collectors commonly report they heard the story from a parent or grandparent who heard it from someone else. This means most dates below could be reduced by *at least* 50 years and in most cases the same version of the tale was being told in that culture.

Cultural and National Variants as Identified by the Collectors and Year of Collection/Publication

1812-1900	Hausa/Nigeria	Kabyl/Algeria	**1961-1970**
African-American/U.S.	Kamba/Kenya	New Mexico	Cameroon
Czecho-Slovak/	Persia	Ngoni/Malawi	Mexico
Czechoslovakia	Russia	Spain	Sierra Leone
France		Suriname	Yoruba/Nigeria
Germany	**1921-1930**	Yiddish	
Greece	African-American		**1971-1980+**
Madagascar	British West Indies	**1941-1950**	Palestinian-Arab
Melanesia	Cape Verde Islands	Argentina	Haiti
Russia	India	Baganda/Uganda	Korea
Scotland	Jamaica	Haiti	Manipur/India
Xhosa/South Africa	Korea	Japan	Rajasthan/India
	Palestine	Pennsylvania Dutch/U.S.	Russia
1901-1910	Puerto Rico		Taiwan
Hausa/Nigeria	Solomon Islands	**1951-1960**	Uganda
Jamaica		France	Yiddish-Canadian
Masai/Kenya	**1931-1940**	Korea	Zulu/Zimbabwe
Mordvin/Russia	Antilles	Kurdistani-Jew	
	Dahomey	Nigeria	
1911-1920	France	Roumania	
Bahamas	French-Missouri/U.S.		
Embu/Kenya			

No matter where or when a tale was collected it was there to be collected because the teller wanted to share it, having heard it from someone else who also loved it and wanted to pass it on. The teller, writes folklorist Carl-Herman Tillhagen, is like "a gardener who selects from many wild flowers those he specially loves, cares for them and cultivates them, and thus grows more beautiful and durable species which he transmits to posterity" (1969, 377). The 35 tales in *A Knock at the Door* await your selection and cultivation.

One Tale around the World

A Telling Look at Pictures

Illustrators, like storytellers, are interpretive artists. They share the goal of bringing a folktale to life by stimulating the audience's re-creation of the story. Where the teller has voice and gesture, the illustrator works with color and line. Where the teller has tone or attitude, the illustrator has style and medium of illustration. Both must make decisions regarding characterization and pacing. The illustrator, however, is governed by physical format. Depending on a book's purpose and design, the illustrator may be required to distill the tale into a single major image or a few key images. Only in the picture book genre does the illustrator have the full interpretive range of the teller. Examining such visual interpretations that artists have created for "The Wolf and the Seven Little Kids" has much to offer the teller of the same tale. At the least such an exploration affirms the range of possible interpretations. At best, it may help the teller see new layers in the story and, in turn, enhance the telling.

"The Wolf and the Seven Little Kids" is most often published as one of many tales in a collection, just as it was in the first edition of the Grimms' *Kinder- und Hausmärchen* in 1812. Illustrators are restricted to one, perhaps two images. Some artists focus on the physical action of the tale while others concentrate on the tale's emotions. A blending of both becomes the most resonant approach.

Thomas Bewick, Gustave Dore, and Marc Chagall have all symbolized the story in fable form by illustrating the primary point of conflict—the wolf and the kid on opposite sides of the same door. Jean de Grandville's illustration manages to contain both the mother's warning and the point of crisis. The mother goat and kid are on opposite sides of the door as she prepares to leave, but the wolf is already lurking nearby.

Artists have a much wider range of actions and emotions to illustrate when working with the folktale version of this same story. That range, however, brings the need to select which scenes are most representative of the tale's experience. Naturally, different artists select different scenes.

Walter Crane's visual interpretation echoes the moral of the fable—heed your mother's warnings. In both editions of *Household Stories*—(1882 with geese and 1886 with goats) Crane depicts the mother telling her children to keep the door locked till she returns. Just below in the elaborate box of the first letter of the story the wolf sits waiting for his chance. Like de Grandville, Crane immediately pulls his audience into the story by establishing the character's innocence and the coming danger.

Wanda Gag's two images in *More Tales from Grimm* (1947) focus on innocence and loss. In the first image the audience shares the kids' perspective as they look up—about to make their fateful decision—at the paw in the door's window. Even with Gag's relaxed, rounded line it is a scene of tension. Her second scene shares the resulting loss of the kids' decision. Mother Goat has just entered the house to find it ravaged and her children gone. The scene is blurred and overwhelming, a moment of grief and horror.

Grimms' Fairy Tales (1968) with an introduction by Frances Clarke Sayers is illustrated by the young winners of a worldwide contest. It offers an interesting contrast to Gag's two scenes of tension and grief. Here the youngest kid's moment of triumph is the visual essence of the interpretation. The mother has already seen the devastation and is just turning to see the surviving kid poking his head out of the clock case. It is a moment of joy within the loss, and hope and survival fill the page. Hot pinks and oranges contribute to the vibrant mood as does the illustrator's naturally naive style. That judges selected this illustration may indicate what they felt the child's perspective ought to be, but seven-year-old Soon Hwa Lee of Korea selected her content and colors without any influence from them.

Recovery, revenge, and the all-protecting role of mother are blended to create the essence of the tale in editions illustrated by Ruth Koser-Michaels and Fritz Kredel in their respective editions, *Marchen du Bruder Grimm* (1937) and *Grimms' Fairy Tales* (1937). Both depict the mother goat with scissors in hand and the youngest kid hiding behind her skirt as they approach the sleeping wolf. These scenes are as much about the coming moments as the current one. A few seconds more and the scissors will cut, the kids will be freed, and revenge will be done. Suspense and bravery fill the image. Kredel's illustration is especially evocative. His characters are clearly living the story, experiencing it as it happens rather than walking through the tale like puppets.

Kredel's mother goat has already rolled up her sleeves. She knows, as does the audience, there is serious work to be done. The audience knows it is dangerous work, too, from the way she's bending so carefully over the wolf and asking for quiet, having placed her hand to her lips. Many illustrators depict the mother cutting open the wolf or about to cut, but their scenes all evoke the danger of going to the market. Kredel's air of danger makes the mother goat's action more heroic. She is rising to the occasion and risking herself to save her children.

Two final examples of single illustrations for "The Wolf and the Seven Little Kids" point to the differences between artists (and tellers) who focus on surface action and those who focus on emotional essence. For Pantheon's long-standard edition, *The Complete Grimms' Fairy Tales* (1944), Josef Scharl chose to illustrate only the wolf. He is not lurking, a sign of action to come, or even sleeping as the mother goat prepares to cut him open. Scharl's wolf has already been filled with stones and stitched back up. Rather than evoking any part of the goats' emotional journey, this image becomes a tabloid photo of a villain waiting for the gallows.

Nonny Hogrogian's etching for the collection *About Wise Men and Simpletons* (1971) translated by Elizabeth Shub offers a rich contrast to Scharl's image. Hogrogian's illustration of the mother goat nuzzling her kids could be the beginning or the end of the story. Motherly love, protection, and family are the essential theme. Yet, even in this relatively passive illustration the audience sees that the door is locked and one kid has a mischievous look in his eyes. It is not a picture of sweetness that holds little life or interest, but one of warmth as it acknowledges the dangers. Hogrogian's fluid line and soft beige paper also contribute (like the teller's voice) to the audience's sense of warmth and involvement. The page is quiet and sure, pulling the audience into the safety of home.

Combining or linking the various single illustrations used in anthologies reveals the tale's primary emotional points or chords. These serve the tale and artist/teller much like musical chords serve the song and singer. The safety of mother and home. Danger at the door. Rescue and revenge. Collections allowing the illustrator a greater number of images, yet not as many as a picture book, begin with these same chords and add the most dramatic scene of all—the wolf bursting into the house. With this image the dramatic arc of the story is complete, and the contrast between images intensifies them all. Balanced against the early images of mother and home and the upcoming images of rescue and home, this scene is horrific, but not overwhelming.

Evgeny Rachev's illustrations in the collection *The Little Clay Hut* (1975) published by what was then the Soviet Union are a fine example of illustrating the tale's full emotional journey. Rachev opens with a small image of home. Next comes a full-page illustration showing mother and kids dressed in peasant smocks and smiling by the fire. This domesticity is destroyed suddenly with the turn of a page. Unexpectedly, the wolf bursts in from the *right* side of the page. The audience is as jarred as the kids who are trying to hide. This physical or visual jolt destroys the calm as does a storyteller's sudden burst of voice and rapid speech. The audience is no longer merely watching the story, but living it. A need for regaining a sense of calm keeps the audience involved in the search for a resolution. Rachev's fourth and final illustration is another doublespread. The clever mother goat stands firmly in the upper right corner watching the wolf (far left) run toward the fire in the middle. The scene is as full as the wolf.

A Telling Look at Pictures

Within seconds the wolf will meet his doom and the kids will be freed. It sparks the audience into imagining the end.

Feodor Rojankovsky follows the same arc of action and emotion in *The Tall Book of Nursery Tales* (1944). Particularly effective is the way Rojankovsky literally places the audience in the role or perspective of the little kids. His wolf jumps through the door at the audience as well as the kids in a moment of direct confrontation. Soft colors and peasant-style designs fill Rojankovsky's scenes of goat-family life, evoking a sense of time past, a safe time because of its distance from a more troubled now.

Herbert Leupin illustrates the same sequence of scenes as Rachev and Rojankovsky in *Grimms' Marchen* (1950), but his tone is very different, which changes the audience's experience of the tale. Leupin uses the cartoon style of severe flat colors and stiff line so frequent in the 1940s. The characters have become cartoon puppets. The threat of the wolf is reduced to Tom's threat toward Jerry the mouse. With the characters in no true danger there is no reason for the audience to enter the tale. It has no one to care for or become. Little but surface action and antics remain.

Leupin's mother goat is so sweet in her tiny hat, wire-rimmed glasses, umbrella, and pocketbook she can't be real. The kids pose like cutouts waiting to decorate a toddler's wall. The wolf, depicted with a safety-pinned coat, cigarette, and liquor bottle, turns the story into melodrama. Campy organ music is playing everywhere. Even the image of the mother goat's grief is void of deep feeling. Rather than a moment of despair, it becomes a badly acted parody of Munch's "The Scream." The most intense image in Leupin's interpretation is that of the wolf asleep, full of kids and an empty liquor bottle at his side. The mother goat is so close to piercing his skin with her scissors there's a dent in his belly. Yet, even here, the characters are walking through the story rather than living it. Such a cartoon interpretation, be it verbal or visual, is certainly as valid as any other, but the interpretive artist can't expect a strong involvement from the audience when it's given so little to work with.

Susan Varley's images for *The Fox and the Cat: Animal Tales from Grimm* told by Kevin Crossley-Holland (1985) begin on a different chord than most editions—the evilness of the wolf. Tucked within a double-spread of text, Varley's first scene is a small image of the wolf threatening the miller. Varley's next and dominant scene is also different than most. Like Gag, she bypasses the violent scene of the wolf leaping through the door and focuses on the mother's experience of finding her home destroyed and her children gone. On one hand, this could be viewed as focusing on the parental experience in the story rather than that of the terrified kids. But honoring the mother's grief may also be viewed as an affirming act of love for the seven little kids whose role the audience is sharing.

Like Kredel's mother goat, Varley's is living the scene and story. She stands at the door, her hand still on the knob. The weight and pain of the empty room is a nightmare come true. Her children are not just gone. The broken furniture, strewn toys, and pillow stuffing about the room tell her and the audience that her children fought for their lives and lost. Weeping, she has picked up one of their rag dolls.

To have made this the last illustration for the story would have made it a tragedy as some folk variants do. Varley, however, is illustrating the Grimm variant and is able to balance the darkness with a vibrant scene of rescue and revenge. The mother goat is stitching up the wolf with an exhilarating grin on her face as the kids watch with eager eyes. The family is alive and taking charge of its world again. There is no need to see the wolf actually drop down the well.

One of the reasons Varley's interpretation is so alive and evocative is that she honors the tale's primary emotional chords. The results of failing to attend to these chords are apparent in Barbara Freeman's illustrations in *Tales from Grimm* translated by W.K. Holmes (1957). Freeman begins with the familiar image of impending danger and includes an illustration of the wolf bursting into the house as goslings run for cover. But from there her emotional connection with the tale fizzles out. The dominant image of her four illustrations, it is in ways her weakest and certainly the least emotional or dramatic. The wolf in elegant attire stands by the river bank while the mother and her goslings wait for him to get thirsty and drown while taking a drink. But the wolf looks to be in fine shape. The image tells the audience nothing of past events and, being so sweet, it tells nothing of events to come. The characters are all but expressionless. In spending so much time on an image that does not evoke or propel the story forward, Freeman loses her audience as surely as a teller who digresses into a detailed description while leaving the characters and action on hold.

The contrasting illustrative interpretations of Raymond Briggs and Svend Otto offer the storyteller additional insights into how best to share a story. In *The Fairy Tale Treasury* selected by Virginia Haviland (1972) Briggs frames the six pages of text with nine scenes from the story. All the emotional chords are included: safety of home and mother, danger at the door, wolf breaking into the house, and the rescue of the kids. In this case it is the placement or pacing of these images that becomes important. Not all scenes or chords in a tale carry the same emotional weight. While Briggs includes illustrations of the wolf eating chalk and talking to the baker, he has made certain that the largest image on the page and the one nearest the turn of the page is one with the little kids staring at the wolf's flour-covered paws in the window. The tension is set and the turn of the page—like the turn of the doorknob—brings chaotic disaster. A full color illustration literally bursting off the edges of the doublespread comes next. It is the moment parents have been warning against for centuries and one that screams with surprise and danger as kids and wolf dart about the room.

In *The Best of Grimms' Fairy Tales* translated by Anthea Bell and Anne Rogers (1979), Svend Otto encounters one of the storyteller's primary problems in pacing—too much too soon and too much of the same. The basic emotional chords are present, but the illustrator has included so many other notes in so little space that the images and emotions chatter all over the pages. And with so many little scenes in one doublespread often depicting different actions it is difficult for any scene to claim more value or resonance than another. In the end it all turns into a monotone.

Illustrators of picture book editions of folktales have the most in common with storytellers. Like the storyteller, the picture book illustrator must honor the tale's primary emotional chords *and* keep the quieter connective scenes alive as well. Four picturebook interpretations of "The Wolf and the Seven Little Kids" offer a look at extreme variations in tone, style, pacing, and the different levels of intimacy between tale, teller, and audience these variations create.

Chris Conover's *Mother Goose and the Sly Fox* (1989) is a curious trip through the looking glass. While Svend Otto crowded his few pages with too much conflicting action, Conover brings the story to a standstill by the way she uses more pages. The problem is not with Conover's elaborate Dutch scenery and costumes. It's that, in the end, they are all she offers her audience. Her visual interpretation is rarely in touch with the tale's emotional arc. And, as a result, her interpretation holds little truth, and few points of entrance for the audience. Time and again she tosses off the tale's primary chords with a small illustration only to focus on a doublespread scene of inaction. Just when the story begs to move forward Conover stops to rest. By continually disgressing she undercuts the very tale she is working to share. The largest illustrations focus on the fox's house, a general landscape with the fox, the fox walking through town, the fox sleeping, and finally, Mother Goose and her goslings swimming home. The geese don't even stay to make sure the fox meets his demise. By its conclusion *Mother Goose and the Sly Fox* has become little more than a folder of pretty pictures with a distant relationship to the text.

Janet Stevens' illustrations for *Nanny Goat and the Seven Little Kids* retold by Eric Kimmel (1990) is told or interpreted in a very different voice than Conover's. Stevens strikes all the tale's emotional chords while propelling the story forward. The scene of the wolf coming through the door explodes full force—too big and too fast to be confined by the pages. As enjoyable as this edition is, it would be more involving if Stevens had been able to settle on a more unified tone or approach. Kimmel's text is relatively direct and serious. But Stevens' images straddle folklore, realism, and parody. Her wolf is pure caricature. With his eyes patch and T-shirt stating "Big and Bad" he is more hollow punk than dangerous villain. Stevens mixes perspectives on the kids as well. Drawn in a relatively realistic style, she then props them up on their hind legs and dresses them in bits of human clothing. Rather than cartoon or anthropomorphic animals (like Arnold Lobel's) these kids remain real goats awkwardly posed like the photographic stories for children so popular in the nineteenth century.

Stevens' use of contemporary details is also problematical. The process of folklore frequently creates contemporary versions or parodies of well-known tales that are spiced with references to jargon and technology clearly outside of "once upon a time." With parody interpretations the purpose and pleasure of the telling are the break in tone. The juxtaposition of folktale and contemporary life is consistent throughout the tale. Because Kimmel's text is not parodic, Stevens' "hip" touches create a game of "I spy," at times gaining more of the audience's attention than the emotional experience at the heart of the tale.

Mrs. Goat and Her Seven Little Kids by Tony Ross (1990) is a comic interpretation in the realm of the film *Home Alone*. Everything is skewed from voice to plot twists. The point and fun of this edition are all the differences and irreverence. When Mrs. Goat warns her kids about the wolf, the youngest vows to "kick him in the foot." When the wolf sticks his paw through the mail slot for identification, one of the kids whacks it with a hammer. The audience doesn't need to worry about the kids. It's the pathetic wolf that gains the audience's attention as it wonders what indignity will strike him next. Even the warm reunion at the end has a comic kick in the pants. After saving her kids and hugging them close Mrs. Goat gives them a whack upside the head for opening the door.

Like Stevens' kids, Ross' have Walkmans and skateboards, etc., but Ross' goats are clearly cartoon goats. Everyone is a caricature. His interpretation has both feet planted on slapstick bananas and he plays all the tale's chords with a banjo's plucky zeal. Colors are bright and loose. Lines are quick and quirky. The entire book is told in the spirit of the typical final chord—a jubilant celebration of the wolf's stupidity and their own cleverness.

Felix Hoffman's illustrations for his 1958 picture book edition of *The Wolf and the Seven Little Kids* are masterful in their completeness and sureness of voice. Where Ross' edition played the tale's chords with a banjo's kenetic strum, Hoffman's is played with the sustaining bow of a cello with each chord building and blending with the next. His muted, earthen colors and ragged style of line and color application all work to evoke the cello's richly textured timbre. Confident of his voice, Hoffman is never compelled to crowd a scene or rush a sequence. More than any other interpreter of this tale he trusts the inherent rhythms and emotions of the story.

Hoffman's opening scene is the essence of all the family has and, as a result, has to lose. The kids are playing in the unfenced yard as their mother watches protectively from a distance. Their little house rests safely on the horizon, but not that far away stands the forest of darkness and wolves. Throughout the book, doublespread illustrations share equal visual weight with the text and begin to subtly build the narrative's tension. Hoffman has no need for larger-than-life action or bold colors. His kids are a smooth blend of realism and fantasy. By turn they walk as goats and then on hind legs as anthropomorphized animals. Hoffman succeeds at this while others flounder for two reasons. His expressionistic style itself evokes a transformed sense of reality and his anthropomorphism is grounded in body and facial expressions rather than physical objects. He trusts the posture and faces of his characters to share the story. Mother is firm, but tender. The kids are proud of being trusted to be on their own and eager to please by following directions. Hoffman's characters breathe like the pages themselves—giving time and space for the audience to enter. An excellent example is the doublespread that illustrates the text: "So the mother goat, bleating happily, went on her way." Mother goat is at the far left side of the image. As if a film camera, Hoffman pans across a long expanse of empty space and silence to the kids at the far right side of the page. In experiencing the visual silence the audience feels the kids' new sense of isolation as well as their pride at being left alone.

Once the door is locked Hoffman's focus on the next four doublespread pages is the wolf's attempts to get inside and his trips to town to alter his voice and appearance. Unable to see the kids, the audience begins to wonder more about them. When the wolf is at the door and showing his flour-covered paws Hoffman switches to the same scene from the kids' point of view. What the kids see matches the truth they've been told to obey, but by first showing the full wolf Hoffman has emphasized the kids' plight—the limited scope of their information and reasoning. And with the kids so thoroughly unaware of the impending danger the audience once again steps into the story through its concern.

In the turn of a page the wolf bursts into the house and kids scramble for safety. The final violence of their being devoured occurs off screen. Like Varley in *The Fox and the Cat*, Hoffman knows the power of letting the aftermath tell of the violence. The mother's grief is all but overwhelming as she surveys her ravaged and childless home. Hoffman's mother doesn't leap into rescuing and revenge with the quickness of a cartoon animal or super hero. Her sense of loneliness and loss is shared through her image alone on an empty, silent page. She is numb as she cradles her sole remaining child. It is only when she accidentally comes upon the sleeping wolf that hope returns. Hope brings action and the mother is confident once again. Two doublespreads show the wolf being cut open, kids freed, and them replacing their weight with stones. The mother, once again the archetypal mother of protection, is handily stitching the wolf closed. Rising to the occasion, the mother becomes more heroic than had she leapt to an easy and quick revenge.

One of the strongest elements in Hoffman's interpretation is the immediacy of each scene and its richness of texture. All chords are honored for their part in the story's song and all played as if for the first time, rich with life's complexity. A fine example of this is the image of the goat's waiting for the wolf to drown. Hoffman features the wolf, but the goats are peeking from the protection of their window. The kids are gleeful at their trick on the trickster. The mother watches with concern.

She knows they are not yet safe—that the story could still go in any direction. But as soon as the wolf leans to drink the story races to its conclusion as Hoffman's images rush ahead. In nearly one beat the wolf falls down the well and the goats dance in reverie—the mother's face and shoulders filled with relief. It is Hoffman's single crowded scene and appropriately so.

Folktales often have verbal framing devices to establish a sense of closure and completeness. Hoffman ends his visual telling with a similar balance by drawing a variation of his opening scene of familial joy and safety. After their harrowing day all seven kids are snuggled in bed. The gentle, full (reborn) moon shines through their window as the mother goat looks down on them. Kids and audience are enveloped in the assurance and protection of the scene.

More than any of the other illustrators discussed here Hoffman knows that chords in song or story don't simply follow one another, but continually evolve, each into the next. Like the music evoked by the cellist's ever-flowing bow, Hoffman's interpretation of "The Wolf and the Seven Little Kids" is an unified whole, enveloping in its modulation.

As these picturebooks reveal, the equality of a tale's interpretation, be it visual or verbal, does not depend on its tone or voice, but on the sureness of that tone and the voice's ability to involve the audience. Does the interpretive artist leave the audience in the distant spectator's role, or does the artist evoke the tale's emotions within the audience, causing them to join with the characters and live the tale? As W.B. Yeats wrote of the arts, the measure of their greatness "can be but in their intimacy" (Yeats, 1961, 224). It is only when tale, teller, and audience blend as one that a tale is fully shared and alive.

ILLUSTRATORS

Bewick, Thomas. *The Fables of Aesop and Others*. London: Longman, 1818.

Briggs, Raymond. *The Fairy Tale Treasury*. Selected by Virginia Haviland. New York: Coward, 1972.

Chagall, Marc. *Fables* by Jean de la Fontaine. Paris: Teriade, 1952.

Conover, Chris. *Mother Goose and the Sly Fox.* New York: Farrar, 1989.

Crane, Walter. *Household Stories.* Translated by Lucy Crane. London: Macmillan, 1882.

Dore, Gustave. *The Fables of La Fontaine.* Translated into English verse by Walter Thornbury. London: Cassell, Petter & Galpin, 1868.

Freeman, Barbara. *Tales from Grimm.* Translated by W.K. Holmes. London: Blackie & Son, 1957.

Gag, Wanda. *More Tales from Grimm.* New York: Coward, 1947.

Grandville, J.J. *Fables of La Fontaine.* Translated from the French by Elizur Wright, Jr. Boston: Tappan & Dennet, 1841.

Hoffman, Felix. *The Wolf and the Seven Little Kids.* New York: Harcourt, [1957] 1959.

Hogrogian, Nonny. *About Wise Men and Simpletons.* Translated by Elizabeth Shub. New York: Macmillan, 1971.

Koser-Michaels, Ruth. *Marchen Du Bruder Grimm.* Munchen: Druemersche, 1937.

Kredel, Fritz. *Grimms' Fairy Tales.* New York: Stackpole, 1937.

Leupin, Herbert. *Grimms' Marchen.* Zurich: Globi-Verlag, 1950.

Rachev, Evgeny. *The Little Clay Hut: Russian Folk Tales about Animals.* Translated by Irina Zheleznova et al. USSR: Progress Publishers, 1975.

Rojankovsky, Feodor. *The Tall Book of Nursery Tales.* New York: Harper, 1944.

Ross, Tony. *Mrs. Goat and Her Seven Little Kids.* New York: Atheneum, 1990.

Scharl, Josef. *The Complete Grimms' Fairy Tales.* New York: Pantheon, 1944.

Soon, Hwa Lee. *Grimms' Fairy Tales.* Based on the Frances Jenkins Olcott edition of the English translation by Margaret Hunt. With an introduction by Frances Clarke Sayers. Chicago: Follett, 1968.

Stevens, Janet. *Nanny Goat and the Seven Little Kids.* Retold by Eric A. Kimmel. New York: Holiday, 1990.

Svend Otto. *The Best of Grimms' Fairy Tales.* Translated by Anthea Bell and Anne Rogers. New York: Larousse, 1979.

Varley, Susan. *The Fox and the Cat: Animals Tales from Grimm.* Retold by Kevin Crossley-Holland. New York: Lothrop, 1985.

Telling with the Current: Helping Children and Folktales Teach Themselves

Making Connections

There are many ways of sharing folktales and interweaving them with students' daily lives and learning. Educators continue to find new activities that make units on folktales and multicultural studies more participatory. (A bibliography of representative sources follows this essay.) These activities and predirected discussions about folktales certainly have their place. But stories connect with our daily lives in activating ways simply by being told. Teachers, librarians, and tellers simply by nurturing these natural connections can help students begin to teach themselves.

After a story is told to students other adults will often compliment the teller by saying, "You certainly kept them still and quiet." This is true but only on the outside. The students were still and quiet because they were so active on the inside. Their minds were not only comparing and contrasting the events of the story with their own lives but also with other stories.

Our Own Experiences and Folktales

When we listen to a story one of the ways to give it meaning is by drawing on our own experiences. These may be events, places, objects, sounds, or even tastes. Each of us has a personalized weave of memories from which to draw. A given tale such as "Cinderella" may touch several points in our memory. We may recall the time, when as children, we were forced to clean our room while siblings were free to play outdoors. The castle and ball we visualize are based on our memory of movies. And when the clock strikes midnight we live Cinderella's pain as we remember times we had to leave parties and friends before we wanted to. At the same time our life validates the tale, the tale validates our feelings, our life. These points of con-

nection are at the core of how and why we remember certain folktales and others fade from memory.

Once a tale has been heard and becomes part of our memory serendipitous connections may continue to occur. It may be something as simple as walking over a wooden bridge and having the sound of footsteps bring to mind the trip-trap-trip-trap of "Three Billy Goats Gruff." It may also be as dramatic as a late night knock at the door bringing to mind "The Wolf and the Seven Little Kids" and our making sure we secure the chain guard before opening the door. It may also be as poetic as seeing the rising moon and remembering the Korean tale of its origin—"The Sun and the Moon."

Exposure to tales is the key ingredient in making these connections occur, exposure without fanfare or lecture so that the tales can be absorbed as stories and entertainment rather than something that feels like it ought to be learned.

Bringing the Tales into Daily Life

One valuable way to share the stories in *A Knock at the Door* is to read all the tales to one's self and then trust the natural manner of people, stories, and memory. Let the stories come forth during the school year whenever something brings a particular tale to mind. Let yourself teach—share—these tales with the flow of things rather than doing what so often feels like swimming upstream.

A Yearlong Unit of Making Connections

You can keep the plan for this type of naturalized, yearlong unit to yourself or let the class know about the book and that you'll be curious to see how many stories come to mind during the year.

In upper-level classes—fourth grade and above—you could even make the stories available to groups of students and let them be in charge of pointing out connections.

Sparks that call certain tales to mind may be large or small. Since gathering these tales together I have experienced various tales coming to mind, each triggered by a different kind of experience. The names of the countries or cultures now leap up as if in bold type whenever I see them. Knowing that these tales have been shared by people turns geographic place names and encyclopedia data into faces.

While reading of South Africa's political unrest I noticed that Nelson Mandela spoke Xhosa as a child. Immediately I thought of the Xhosa tale, "The Story of Demane and Demazana." Did Mandela, I wondered, hear this version as a child just as I heard "The Wolf and the Seven Little Kids"? Through this connection Mandela evolved from a national and seemingly distant figure into a fellow man with a past filled with stories.

Another time I turned over a handmade greeting card and discovered it was from Madagascar. Before reading the tale "Indesoka" I would have simply glanced at the place name and forgotten it. But being familiar with "Indesoka," the name was no longer just a faraway place. It had become a place of people and stories that share my classic uneasiness at the knock at the door *and* my joy at the victim's survival.

A television report on the devastating effect of AIDS on adults in Uganda felt, somehow, even more personal by my knowing "The Grandmother and the Apes." As I sat listening to the numbers of children who are losing both parents to AIDS I kept wondering who will tell them this story, tell them any stories? Do they even have a grandmother? Do they think of the tale in which children save adults as they sit unable to help their own parents with AIDS?

A book on my parents' shelf about the Pennsylvania Dutch has been there for years. Now the sight of it brings to mind "The Rabbit and the Bear." But more than just the tale comes to mind. Since first reading the tale my eyes have become more likely to notice references to the Pennsylvania Dutch in whatever I read. The natural process

of story connections becomes a growing spiral. The tale makes me notice things related to the tale's culture. And what I notice from the tale's culture brings to mind the tale *and* all I've learned about the culture so far.

As adults working with children we can let our personal connections such as those I've experienced lead to our times of telling certain tales. But just as many or more connections will evolve within the classroom and have a more immediate tie with the children's lives.

Current Events and Folktales

Current events—local or international—may bring a tale to mind. Ants or wasps in the classroom, upsetting students, can spark a telling of insects who helped in tales like "The Three Kids" (Cape Verde Islands), "The Rabbit and the Bear" (Pennsylvania Dutch: U.S.), and "The Story of Demane and Demazana" (Xhosa: South Africa).

Worldwide events are just as likely to create moments for sharing certain tales. The 1992 Olympics involved people (and as a result, stories) from around the world, especially France and Spain. Television coverage of events might well have sparked times for telling "The Goat, the Kids, and the Wolf" (France) and "Carlanco" (Spain). Aesop is also connected to the Olympics with his fable "The Kid and the Wolf," which dates back to the time of the original Olympics in Greece.

Middle-East peace talks go on and on in fits and starts. But behind the leaders seen on television are thousands of people living, working, and telling tales. By sharing tales such as "The Little She-Goat" (Palestinian-Arab) and "The Ewe, the Goat and the Lion" (Kurdistani-Jew), students begin to see and experience similarities even between extremes and angry diversity. They begin to see similarities between warring cultures and also between those cultures *and* our own, which loves to tell "The Wolf and the Seven Little Kids."

The Child's World and Folktales

The local and common can also spark times for sharing certain tales. A child's or a class's preoccupation with monsters opens the door for monstrous creatures in several tales. "A Father's Children" (Kamba: Kenya), "The Golden Chain from Heaven" (Japan), "The Girl and the Tiger-Man" (Manipur: India), and others feature monsters that could give Freddie Kreuger and Bigfoot a run for their money and popularity. "Tagaro's Fish" (Vanuatu) may come to mind when a student proudly describes his or her new aquarium or any new pet. References to a treehouse and secret passwords in a novel you are reading aloud to the class can open the door for telling a tale like "The Monkey and the Hyena" (Ngoni: Malawi). Clearly, the sparks and possibilities for telling are endless.

Integrating Folktales into the Curriculum

Part of the child's daily environment is also the ongoing curriculum, which is filled with sparks for telling tales. Sharing folktales can help bring life and emotion to the people who lived the dates and statistics that so often dominate textbooks.

Social Studies and Folktales

The history of North America (like so many other areas) is based on a blend of invasion and immigration. "The Three Kids" (Cape Verde Islands) and "The Rabbit and the Bear" (Pennsylvania Dutch: U.S.) both came to North America in the memories of people who chose to move to the United States. Jews from eastern Europe, one of many ethnic groups emigrating to Canada, brought their version of the same tale called "A Granny Who Had Many Children." Other versions of the tale, such as "The Cunning Snake" (African-American: U.S.), were brought by people who were captured and relocated against their will as slaves.

The subject of slavery itself stretches in several directions that connect with tales in *A Knock at the Door* and far beyond the U.S. Civil War. The Embu of Kenya who were chased and captured as slaves on the east coast of Africa tell a tale of surviving enslavement titled "The Goat and the Kids and the Bogey." And what of the men and women who were taken from Africa to the Caribbean and forced to work on the sugar plantations so that our great-grandparents could sweeten their coffee?

Their lives may have included "Tiger Softens His Voice" (Jamaica) and "The Devil Hammers His Tongue" (Grenada). At the same time that politics and bigotry tear people apart, folklore binds them together. Encourage students to imagine if those held as slaves and those who held them ever realized they shared a story.

The Arts and Folktales

Just as history means people, so do arts and crafts. Beautiful Persian carpets were made by people who may have known "The Story of the Wolf and the Goat" (Persia). Haiku poems may spark thoughts of Japanese tales. Let students imagine whether Japanese Haiku poets Issa and Basho might have known "The Golden Chain from Heaven." What French versions of this same tale might have been known by the painter Claude Monet? Perhaps Michaelangelo knew one of the early fable versions. Through sharing these tales, writers and artists who so easily seem beyond our comprehension and daily lives are seen anew as people like us whose lives are filled with stories. People like us who hear stories and automatically make connections with their memories and surroundings.

Language Arts and Folktales

As family reunions prove time and again, nothing sparks a story like another story being told. The same is true with folktales. Language arts curricula open numerous doors for sharing tales. "Cinderella," for example, whether read or told or seen as a film, can easily lead to other French tales, including "The Goat, the Kids and the Wolf" or La Fontaine's retelling in fable form, "The Wolf and the Kid." Sharing John Steptoe's award-winning book, *Mufaro's Beautiful Daughters* (1987), can lead to sharing other Xhosa tales such as "The Story of Demane and Demazana."

Elements of a story in addition to culture or geography can spark other stories as well. Children are quick to identify familiar special objects or plot patterns in folktales. Share Nonny Hogrogian's picturebook retelling of the Armenian tale *One Fine Day* (1971) and then "The Little She-Goat" (Palestinian-Arab), and the child will comment on how stories are alike—their common feature being a cumulative plot where an animal goes from character to character with each demanding something in return until they form a chain of requests and bequeaths. Tagaro calls his fish to the surface of the water for conversation in "Tagaro's Fish" (Vanuatu) and so does the fisherman in "The Fisherman's Wife." The house of the Tiger Witch in "The Tiger Witch" (Taiwan) is made of sweets like the witch's house in "Hansel and Gretel." The Hausa tale, "Journey to the Mending City," shares the same basic story as the Caldecott Honor Book, *The Talking Eggs* told by Robert San Soucci, with illustrations by Brian Pinkney (1989). In both a greedy character tries to copy another's behavior only to meet with disaster and punishment.

As we have seen, language arts lead us naturally to an awareness of our personal relationships with tales. Many excellent novels for young readers bring this fact to life by establishing a character's identity and sense of place by sharing or referring to tales that the character knows. One of the many rich moments of connection between character and reader in Joan Blos's beautiful *A Gathering of Days* (1979) is when the father tells his family the tale of "The Fisherman's Wife." Readers know a bit more about the Wilders and find yet another common bond with the children when Ma tells a drawing-tale in *On the Banks of Plum Creek* (1937). And readers *begin* to understand Joan, as does she herself, in *The Star Fisher* (1991) by Laurence Yep when she tells another character the tale that haunts her thoughts and memories.

Whether the author of a story includes references to specific tales or not, folktales are still a part of a character's life. Pondering what tales a character might know can spark new opportunities to share a tale. And, without making a lesson of it, they help give the tale a sense of context for the child. The children in *The Bicycle Man* by Allen Say (1982) might know "The Golden Chain from Heaven." Did the American soldiers who came to visit that Japanese school know "The Wolf and the Seven Little Kids" or "The Cunning Snake?" Darling, daring Madeline of *Madeline* by Ludwig Bemelmans (1939) most likely heard La Fontaine's fable, "The Wolf and the Kid" from Miss Clavel.

Perhaps those who laughed at Ferdinand in *Ferdinand the Bull* by Leaf and Lawson (1938) had gasped the night before when someone told "Carlanco." Again and again, sparks for telling folktales are everywhere.

Putting Folktales into a Cultural Context

As mentioned above, encouraging children to wonder what tales a fictional character might know helps give the child a sense of context or culture of a tale. But it is only a beginning. If, for example, Madeline *did* hear La Fontaine's fable or the folktale version, "The Goat, the Kids and the Wolf," she would most likely have had a very different listening experience than United States listeners will.

If we look at cultures as large families we can better grasp the difference between Madeline's listening experience and our own. A stranger may enjoy hearing a family story, but that enjoyment can never be as rich as that experienced by a family member. Family members have image-filled memories that enliven the story. They know, for example, about Aunt Ethel's taste in hats and can see the haunted farmhouse mentioned in the story being told. For family members each story is part of a greater whole. For strangers, the same story floats in fuzzy isolation. Folktales told to those of us outside the family or cultural context may suffer a similar isolation.

Without family or cultural information, telling and listening to folktales can become a drab experience. Far worse, it can become a type of literary colonization. Telling folktales is a very visual experience for both teller and listener. Their minds create personalized films of the characters and action, and these internal images can only be based on what they know.

When I was a child in Kansas my mother often told me of "long ago" days when Native Americans lived and traveled on the plains. My mind's eye saw the Indians, but only within *my* context. I imagined them riding down the block (my world at that time) as *I* knew it—asphalt and two-story houses. Part of this can be attributed to childhood innocence, but the syndrome can easily grow into cultural chauvinism. Just as early explorers sought different lands only to remake them in their homeland's image, people often search for foreign tales only to recast them to their own world of images.

Celebrating the Universal *and* the Specific

One of the riches of folklore and a primary goal of *A Knock at the Door* is celebrating the universal in the specific *and* the specific in the universal. Without honoring the specific—cultural and geographical uniqueness—we lessen the resonance of the universal experience. The goal of multicultural studies is not to welcome other peoples because we can remake their tales to match our own but to celebrate our common emotional experiences *through* our differences.

In the ongoing process of folklore, tales do evolve to reflect a culture's home environment. The Japanese, for example, adapted the Chinese and Korean tales, replacing the evil tiger with the Japanese monster, Yamauba, because there are no tigers in Japan. But this represents a natural or organic process involving many people over a period of time, not through one teller's or one listener's need to reshape a tale before it can be accepted or enjoyed.

By increasing students' awareness of the family or culture that surrounds a folktale, the teller/teacher can help students feel more a part of that "family" and as a result, enrich their enjoyment by helping them to literally see more as they hear the story.

Any information that helps place the tale within its daily world enriches the experience for both teller and listener. This does not, however, mean an encyclopedia's list of facts and a follow-up quiz. Nor does it mean oral footnotes in the course of telling a story. A stranger does not become part of a family nor an individual a member of a culture just by memorizing names, places, and dates. Becoming part of a family or beginning to truly see another culture requires time and shared experience. Most of all, it requires an openness.

I do not mean to imply that one can learn or come to understand a culture by simply hearing a folktale or reading a few books and articles. The rich complexities of a culture cannot be reduced or distilled into a few pages or photographs. Such a reduction would also assume that everyone within a given culture is alike. Yet, at the same time, it is important to acknowledge and honor cultural elements by sharing written and visual materials. When we begin to honor the cultural differences or the specific elements, we are then better able to honor the universal or our common bonds.

Resources for Sharing Cultural Information

School and public libraries abound with images that tellers/teachers can leave out and open for students' ongoing exploration and absorption. Magazines like *Faces, Cobblestone,* and *National Geographic* bring the world of folktales into our lives on a regular basis. The November 1991 issue of *Cobblestone,* for example, helps give a sense of time and place to "The Granny Who Had many Children" with its entire issue devoted to "The Story of American Jews." Through that issue's articles and photographs students can begin to put faces and in turn lives to the immigrants who loved this tale and passed it on. The February 1992 issue concentrates on Haiti. "La Belle Venus" gains a new richness for any student who even browses through that issue's pieces on Haitian art, voodoo, and folklore. *National Geographic* offers equally focused background images and information in volume after volume. The February 1981 issue, for instance, shares the world of "La Belle Venus" as well with the featured photo essay, "The Caribbean: Sun, Sea and Seething," by Noel Grove and Steve Raymer.

Books and magazines can certainly be shared directly with tales as part of a teaching unit or teaching style, but, like the tales themselves, they may be most effective when shared, then left for students to explore on their own in their own way and time. Once again this involves trust in the natural course or current of folktales and human memory. And trust in the joy of discovery. Left on their own along with some quiet nurturing most

Telling with the Current

children will follow the same natural path of making connections between tales and self and tales and culture that you find yourself experiencing.

Handsome books filled with photographs and photographs of art wait to be looked through like new and old issues of *Look* and *Life* were by past generations. The more visual experiences students have gathered in their memories, the more they have to draw on while visualizing tales being told.

Wandering through *Traditional Houses of Rural France* (Laws, 1991), to cite an example, can only make "The Goat, the Kids and the Wolf" more vivid in the child's mind. "The Lame Wolf" is given similar enrichment by soaking up the images in *Rajasthan: India's Enchanted Land* (Singh, 1981). Books of art also add life to a tale by sharing a culture's sense of color and shape. Browsing through *Haitian Art* (Stebick, 1978) and *The Wood Architecture of Russia* (Opolovnikov, 1989) either before or after hearing "La Belle Venus" and "The Wolf and the Goat" widens the audience's experience of the tales. Any amount of time spent in the pages of *Jewish Life in Canada* (Kurelek, 1976) helps put faces and homes with those who told "A Granny Who Had Many Children." *Caribbean Canvas* (Lessac, 1987) and *Pennsylvania Dutch: Craftsman and Farmers* (Costabel, 1986) are fine examples of books published for children which also bring folktales to life.

Some important points of caution or understanding must accompany the selection and sharing of these materials. Misguided cultural sharings can be worse than none at all. Cultures of a geographic area, like children of one family, may be similar in many ways, but they are not identical and dislike losing their own identity by being lumped together. Taiwan, for example, is a Chinese country, but it is not the same as the People's Republic of China. To offer books that deal only with mainland China is to ignore Taiwan's unique history and development. The peoples of Africa have endured decades of thoughtless references that spoke of Africa as if it were one country rather than a continent, like Europe, composed of many distinct cultures. A tale such as "Journey to the Mending City" told by the Hausa of Nigeria is from a very different world than that of "The Story of Demane and Demazana," which comes from the Xhosa of South Africa. Their religions, language, land, and histories are distinct from one another.

A second point of caution is balance. Countries and cultures are, for the most part, no more stuck in time than a child. Growth and change are constant. The United States and its people have changed a great deal in the last 100 years. So have the cultures of the folktales we share. *A Century of Japanese Photography* (Downer, 1980) is a wonderful way to evoke a sense of old Japan. But Japan is not *just* past times. It's also high-speed trains and rock and roll. Kimonos and Elvis t-shirts are seen, side by side, on the crowded streets.

The tales and materials are waiting, and the natural current of people and stories is on *your* side. Trust, and the slightest supportive gestures on your part, may bring great results. *Keep* trusting and nurturing students' own connections, and you'll be surprised at how far they'll go in so little time. And into a wider and wider world of understanding and delight in story.

Folktales and Teaching Activities

The following are additional resources that may be helpful for sharing folktales with children.

Barton, Bob, and Booth, David. *Stories in the Classroom: Storytelling, Reading Aloud and Roleplaying with children.* Portsmouth, NH: Heinemann, 1990.

Bauer, Caroline Feller. *Handbook for Storytellers.* Chicago: American Library Association, 1977.

Clarkson, Atelia, and Cross, Gilbert B. *World Folktales: A Scribner Resource Collection.* New York: Scribners, 1980.

Garvie, Edie. *Story As Vehicle: Teaching English to Young Children.* Philadelphia: Multilingual Matters Ltd., 1990.

Maguire, Jack. *Creative Storytelling: Choosing, Inventing, and Sharing Tales for Children.* New York: McGraw-Hill, 1985.

Sierra, Judy, and Kaminski, Robert. *Twice Upon a Time: Stories to Tell, Retell, Act Out, and Write About.* New York: Wilson, 1989.

Resources

Aarne, Antti. *The Types of the Folktale: A Classification and Bibliography.* Translated and enlarged by Stith Thompson. New York: Burt Franklin, [1928] 1971.

Aesop. *Aesop without Morals: The Famous Fables and a Life of Aesop* by Lloyd W. Daily. New York: Thomas Yoseloff, 1961.

———. *Aesop's Fables* by Munro Leaf. Illustrated by Robert Lawson. New York: Heritage Reprints, 1941.

———. *Fables of Aesop.* Translated by Roger L'Estrange. Illustrated by Alexander Calder. New York: Dover, [1931] 1967.

Afanas'ev, Alesksandr. *Russian Fairy Tales.* Translated by Norbert Guterman. New York: Pantheon, 1945.

Ashliman, D.L. *A Guide to Folktales in the English Language.* Westport, CT: Greenwood Press, 1987.

Azzolina, David S. *Tale Type and Motif Indexes: An Annotated Bibliography.* New York: Garland, 1987.

Bachelard, Gaston. *The Poetics of Reverie: Childhood, Language, and the Cosmos.* Translated by Daniel Russell. Boston: Beacon Press, [1960] 1971.

Baer, Florence E. *Sources and Analogues of the Uncle Remus Tales.* Folk Lore Fellows Communications #228. 1980.

Bascom, William. "African Folktales in America." *Research in African Literature.* 13(1981): 181-95.

Beckwith, Martha Warren. *Jamaica Anansi Stories.* (Memoirs of the American Folk-Lore Society, Vol. 17). New York: American Folk-Lore Society, 1924.

Bemelmans, Ludwig. *Madeline.* New York: Viking, 1939.

Blos, Joan W. *A Gathering of Days: A New England Girl's Journal, 1830-32.* New York: Scribners, 1979.

Boedker, Laurits. *Indian Animal Tales.* Folk Lore Fellows Communications #148. 1957.

Boggs, Ralph S. *Index of Spanish Folktales.* Folk Lore Fellows Communications #90. 1930.

Borgohain, B.K., and Chadbury, P.C. Roy. *Folktales of Nagaland, Manipur, Tripura and Mizoram.* New Delhi: Sterling, 1975.

Brendle, Thomas R., and Troxell, William S. "Pennsylvania German Folk Tales, Legends, Once-Upon-a-Time Stories, Maxims and Sayings" in *Pennsylvania German Society: Proceedings and Addresses at Fiftieth Anniversary* (Lancaster, Penn. October 17, 1941). Norristown, PA: Pennsylvania German Society, 1944.

Cabellero, Fernan. *Spanish Fairy Tales.* Philadelphia: Lippincott, n.d.

Cheney, Cora. *Tales from a Taiwan Kitchen.* New York: Dodd, Mead, & Co., 1976.

Chimombo, Steve. *Malawian Oral Literature: The Aesthetics of Indigenous Arts.* Zomba, Malawi: Centre for Social Research, University of Malawi, 1988.

Codrington, Robert H. *The Melanesians: Studies in Their Anthropology and Folk-Lore.* Oxford: Clarendon Press, 1891.

Costabel, Eva. *Pennsylvania Dutch: Craftsman and Farmers.* New York: Atheneum, 1986.

Coxwell, Charles Fillingham. *Siberian and Other Folk Tales: Primitive Literature of the Empire of the Tsar.* London: C.W. Daniel, 1925.

Daly, Lloyd W. *Aesop without Morals: The Famous Fables and a Life of Aesop.* New York: Thomas Yoseloff, 1961.

David, Alfred, and David, Mary Elizabeth. "A Literary Approach to the Brothers Grimm." *Journal of the Folklore Institute.* 1(1964): 180-86.

Dinesh, Kamini. *Folk Tales of Rajasthan.* Jodhpur, India: Jainsons Publications, 1979.

Eastman, Mary Huse. *Index to Fairy Tales, Myths and Legends.* 2nd ed. Boston: F.W. Faxon, 1926.

———. *Index to Fairy Tales, Myths and Legends.* Supplement. Boston: F.W. Faxon, 1937.

———. *Index to Fairy Tales, Myths and Legends.* 2nd Supplement. Boston: F.W. Faxon, 1952.

Eberhard, Wolfram. *Studies in Taiwanese Folktales.* Taipei: Chinese Association for Folklore, 1971.

Elliot, Geraldine. *The Long Grass Whispers.* New York: Schocken, [1939] 1968.

Flowers, Helen. *A Classification of Folktales of the West Indies by Types and Motifs.* New York: Arno Press, 1980.

Fowke, Edith. *Folk Lore of Canada.* Toronto: McClelland and Steward, 1976.

Franzke, Erich. *Fairy Tales in Psychotherapy: The Creative Use of Old and New Tales.* Translated by Joseph A. Smith. Lewiston, NY: Hans Huber Publications, [1985] 1989.

Frobenius, Leo, and Cox, Douglas C. *African Genesis.* New York: Stackpole, 1937.

Gerber, Adolph. *Great Russian Animal Tales.* New York: Burt Franklin, [1891] 1970.

Grimm, Wilhelm and Grimm, Jacob. *The Complete Grimms' Fairy Tales.* Translated by Margaret Hunt. New York: Pantheon, 1944.

Grove, Noel, and Raymer, Steve. "The Caribbean: Sun, Sea and Seething." *National Geographic.* February 1981. p. 244-71.

Hansen, Terrence L. *The Types of the Folktale in Cuba, Puerto Rico, the Dominican Republic and Spanish South America.* Berkeley: University of California Press, 1957.

Haring, Lee. *Malagasy Tale Index.* Folk Lore Fellows Communications #231. 1982.

Harris, Joel Chandler. *Nights with Uncle Remus: Myths and Legends of the Old Plantation* in *The Complete Tales of Uncle Remus.* Boston: Houghton, [1833] 1955.

Ikeda, Hiroko. *A Type and Motif Index of Japanese Folk-Literature.* Folk Lore Fellows Communications #209. 1971.

In-Hak, Choi. *A Type Index of Korean Folktales.* Seoul: Myong Ji University Publishing, 1979.

Jacobs, Joseph. *English Fairy Tales.* London: Putnam, 1988.

"Japan." *Faces.* April 1990. Complete issue.

Japan Photographers Association. *A Century of Japanese Photography.* Introduction by John Dower. New York: Pantheon, 1980.

Jason, Heda. *Types of Indic Oral Tales.* Folk Lore Fellows Communications #242. 1989.

———. "Types of Jewish-Oriental Tales." *Fabula* 7(1965): 115-22.

Johnson, Gyneth. *How Donkeys Came to Haiti and Other Tales.* New York: Devin-Adair, 1949.

Kalibala, E. Balintuma, and Davis, Mary Gould. *Wakaima and the Clay Man and Other African Folk Tales.* New York: Longmans Green, 1946.

Kellery, John E., and Johnson, James H. "Motif-Index Classification and Tales of 'Ysopete Ystoriado.'" *Southern Folklore Quarterly.* 18(1945): 85-117.

Kirtley, Bacil R. *A Motif-Index of Polynesian, Melanesian, and Micronesian Narratives.* New York: Arno Press, 1980.

Klipple, May Augusta. *African Folktales in Foreign Analogues.* Dissertation. University of Indiana, 1938.

Kurelek, William. *Jewish Life in Canada.* With a historical essay by Abraham Arnold. Edmonton, AB: Hurtig, 1976.

La Fontaine, Jean de. *The Fables of La Fontaine.* Translated by Margaret Wise Brown. New York: Harper, 1940.

Laws, Bill. *Traditional Houses of Rural France.* New York: Abbeville, 1991.

Leaf, Munro. *Aesop's Fables.* Illustrated by Robert Lawson. New York: Heritage Reprints, 1941.

———. *Ferdinand the Bull.* Illustrated by Robert Lawson. New York: Viking, 1938.

Lessac, Frane. *Caribbean Canvas.* New York: Lippincott, 1987.

L'Estrange, Roger. *Fables of Aesop.* Illustrated by Alexander Calder. New York: Dover, [1931] 1967.

Lindblom, Gerhard. *Kamba Folklore II, Tales of Supernatural Beings and Adventures.* (Arches D-Etudes Orientales. 20:2). Lund: Berlingska Boktryckeriet, 1935.

Lorimer, D.C.R. *Persian Tales.* London: Macmillan, 1919.

MacDonald, Margaret Read. *The Storyteller's Sourcebook: A Subject, Title and Motif Index to Folklore Collections for Children.* Detroit, MI: Neal-Schuman/Gale Research, 1982.

Marie de France. *Fables.* Edited and translated by Harriet Spiegel. Toronto: University of Toronto Press, 1987.

Massignon, Genevieve, ed. *Folktales from France.* Translated by Jacqueline Hyland. Chicago: University of Chicago Press, 1968.

Muhawi, Ibrahim, and Kanaana, Sharif. *Speak, Bird, Speak Again: Palestinian Arab Folktales.* Berkeley: University of California Press, 1989.

Nemcova, Bozena. *The Disobedient Kids and Other Czecho-Slovak Fairy Tales.* Interpreted by William H. Tomas and V. Smetanka. Selected by Dr. V. Tille. Prague: Koci, 1921.

Neuland, Lena. *Motif Index of Latvian Folktales and Legends.* Folk Lore Fellows Communications #229, 1981.

Nicholson, Jack. "The Rolling Stone Interview" by Fred Shruers. *Rolling Stone.* August 14, 1986. p. 48.

Noy, Dov. *The Jewish Animal Tale of Oral Tradition.* (Israel Folklore Archive Publication Series #29). Haifa: Haifa Municipality, 1976.

Opolovnikov, Alexander, and Opolovnikov, Yelena. *The Wood Architecture of Russia.* New York: Abrams, 1989.

Orde-Browne, Major G. St.J. *The Vanishing Tribes of Kenya*. London: Seeling, 1925. Reprint. Westport, CT: Negro Universities Press, 1970.

Parsons, Elsie Clews. *Folk-Lore from the Cape Verde Islands. Part I*. (Memoirs of the American Folk-Lore Society, Vol. 15). Cambridge, MA: American Folk-Lore Society, 1913.

———. *Folk-Lore of the Antilles, English and French. Part I*. (Memoirs of the American Folk-Lore Society, Vol. 26). New York: American Folk-Lore Society, 1933.

Pellowski, Anne. *The World of Storytelling; Expanded and Revised Edition: A Practical Guide to the Origins, Development and Application of Storytelling*. Bronx, NY: H.W. Wilson, 1990.

Perry, Ben Edwin. *Babrius and Phaedrus*. Cambridge, MA: Harvard University Press, 1965.

Rattray, R. Sutherland. *Hausa Folk-Lore, Customs, Proverbs, Etc. Volume II*. Oxford: Clarendon Press, 1913.

Robe, Stanley L. *Index of Mexican Folktales, Including Narrative Texts from Mexico, Central America and the Hispanic United States*. Berkeley: University of California Press, 1973.

———. *Mexican Tales and Legends from Los Altos*. Berkeley: University of California Press, 1970.

Sabar, Yona. *The Folk Literature of the Kurdistani Jews: An Anthology*. New Haven: Yale University Press, 1982.

Sawyer, Ruth. *Picture Tales from Spain*. New York: Stokes, 1936.

Say, Allen. *The Bicycle Man*. Boston: Houghton-Mifflin, 1982.

Schwarzbaum, Haim. *The Mishle Shu-Alim (Fox Fables) of Rabbi Berechiah ha-Nakdan: A Study in Comparative Folklore and Fable Lore*. Kiron, Israel: Institute for Jewish and Arab Folklore Research, 1978.

———. *Studies in Jewish and World Folklore*. Berlin: Walter de Gruyter and Co., 1968.

Seki, Keigo, ed. *Folktales of Japan*. Translated by Robert J. Adams. Chicago: University of Chicago Press, 1963.

Sibree, James, Jr. "The Oratory, Songs, Legends and Folk-Tales of the Malagasy." *Folk-Lore Journal* 1(1883): 273-77.

Singh, Raghubir. *Rajasthan: India's Enchanted Land*. New York: Thames and Hudson, 1981.

Stebich, Ute. *Haitian Art*. New York: Abrams, 1978.

Steptoe, John. *Mufaro's Beautiful Daughters*. New York: Lothrop, 1987.

"The Story of the American Jews." *Cobblestone*. 12(November 1991): Complete issue.

Suilleabhain, Sean and Christiansen, Reider. *The Types of the Irish Folktale*. Folk Lore Fellows Communications #188, 1963.

Thea,, George McCall. *Kaffir Folk-Lore: A Selection from the Traditional Tales Current among the People Living on the Eastern Border of the Cape Colony*. London: Sonnenschein, 1886. Reprint. Westport, CT: Negro Universities Press, 1970.

Thompson, Stith. *European Tales among the North American Indians: A Study in the Migration of Folk-Tales*. (Colorado College Publication. General Series #100-101. Language Series Volume II, #34) Colorado Springs, CO. April-May, 1919.

———. *The Folktale*. New York: Holt, 1946.

———. *Types of Indic Oral Tales: India, Pakistan and Ceylon*. Folk Lore Fellows Communications #180. 1960.

———. *The Types of the Folktale: A Classification and Bibliography*. 2nd rev. ed. Folk Lore Fellows Communications #184. 1961.

Tillhagen, Carl-Herman. Translated and quoted in *Folktales and Society: Storytelling in a Hungarian Peasant Community* by Linda Degh. Translated by Emily M. Schossberger. Bloomington: Indiana University Press, 1969.

Ting, Nai-Tung. *A Type of Index of Chinese Folktales*. Folk Lore Fellows Communications #223. 1978.

Todd, Loreto. *Some Day Been Day: West African Pidgin Folktales*. London: Routledge and Kegan Paul, 1979.

Tremearne, A.J.N. *Hausa Superstitions and Customs: An Introduction to the Folk-Lore and the Folk*. London: John Bale, 1913.

Wilder, Laura Ingalls. *On the Banks of Plum Creek*. New York: Harper, 1937.

Yeats, W.B. "Certain Noble Plays of Japan." In *Essays and Introductions*. New York: Macmillan, 1961.

Yep, Laurence. *The Star Fisher*. New York: Morrow, 1991.

Zipes, Jack. *Fairy Tales and the Art of Subversion: The Classical Genre for Children and the Process of Civilization*. New York: Wildman Press, 1983.

Zong, In-Sob. *Folktales from Korea*. London: Routledge and Kegan Paul, 1951. Reprint. New York: Grove Press, 1979.

Index

by Janet Perlman

Index   173